The 7 Maxims for Soul Happiness

HOW TO UNLEASH YOUR INNER BLISS

PAUL RODNEY TURNER

BALBOA.
PRESS
A DIVISION OF HAY HOUSE

Balboa Press books may be ordered through booksellers or by contacting:

Balboa Press
A Division of Hay House
1663 Liberty Drive
Bloomington, IN 47403
www.balboapress.com
1 (877) 407-4847

Because of the dynamic nature of the Internet, any web addresses or
links contained in this book may have changed since publication and
may no longer be valid. The views expressed in this work are solely those
of the author and do not necessarily reflect the views of the publisher,
and the publisher hereby disclaims any responsibility for them.

The author of this book does not dispense medical advice or prescribe the use
of any technique as a form of treatment for physical, emotional, or medical
problems without the advice of a physician, either directly or indirectly. The
intent of the author is only to offer information of a general nature to help you
in your quest for emotional and spiritual well-being. In the event you use any
of the information in this book for yourself, which is your constitutional right,
the author and the publisher assume no responsibility for your actions.

Any people depicted in stock imagery provided by Getty Images are
models, and such images are being used for illustrative purposes only.
Certain stock imagery © Getty Images.

Scripture quotations marked (NIV) are taken from the Holy Bible, New
International Version®, NIV®. Copyright © 1973, 1978, 1984, 2011 by Biblica,
Inc.™ Used by permission of Zondervan. All rights reserved worldwide. www.
zondervan.com The "NIV" and "New International Version" are trademarks
registered in the United States Patent and Trademark Office by Biblica, Inc.™

Scripture taken from The Holy Bible, 21st Century King James Version (KJ21®),
Copyright © 1994, Deuel Enterprises, Inc., Gary, SD 57237, and used by permission.

Print information available on the last page.

ISBN: 978-1-9822-2245-1 (sc)
ISBN: 978-1-9822-2246-8 (e)

Balboa Press rev. date: 03/19/2019

Contents

Dedication

I dedicate this book to my very first spiritual mentor, Jeff Cassells. I grew up with Jeff in the poor neighborhood of Whalan, a small town in Sydney's Western suburbs. Jeff and I were both curious boys, and during our early teenage years we took a liking to astronomy and spent many nights studying the stars and philosophizing about the meaning of life. It was Jeff who first pointed me in the right direction when my inquisitiveness led me to ask questions about God. Jeff introduced me to the mystic teachings of India, where I first learned about reincarnation, karma and the real purpose of human life. Jeff was also there when I first experimented with psychedelic drugs and had my first out-of-body experience. If not for Jeff, I don't know what my life would have become, but his sharp and piercing intelligence helped me make decisions early on in life that I believe served me well, and for that, I am forever grateful.

Introduction

Happiness is something we all look for, whether in food, sex, entertainment, relationships, children, career, hobbies or sleep. Happiness drives us, and indeed it defines the quality of our life. One may have immense wealth but if they are not happy, then mostly, they have failed in life.

Without happiness, life loses its value and so with the apparent decrease in satisfaction, we are seeing an increase in suicide all around the world.

In a world where mental and physical stimuli are in abundance, it seems inconceivable that anyone could be unhappy. Surely, everyone can find some form of happiness, but alas, many, many people fail and live their lives sad and exasperated; or hope against hope for some sliver of joy to appear over the horizon of their destiny.

Happiness is the nature of the spirit, as stated in the Vedanta-sutras: *anandamayo 'bhyāsāt* —"the soul, is by nature full of joy."

However, due to misidentifying our true self with matter, we lose touch with this natural blissful state and identify with the pain and suffering of a physical form.

When a soul is entrapped by a material body, it at once identifies with physical relationships and forgets its true identity as a spiritual being. This false ego, influenced by the modes of material nature further entraps the soul in a web of karmic actions and reactions.

While the mind is the instrument for feeling, the intelligence has a deliberative function and can help us navigate our way through the mire of materialism. The intelligent person, therefore, can attain release from the illusion of material existence by the proper use of intelligence.

Vedic scholar and my spiritual mentor, Srila Prabhupada once wrote:

"An intelligent person can detect the awkward position of material existence and thus begin to inquire as to what he is, why he is subjected to different kinds of miseries, and how to get rid of all miseries, and thus, by good association, an advanced intelligent person can turn towards the better life of self-realization."

The "modes material nature" are subtle forces that influence our behavior as well as every aspect of our physical, mental, and emotional experience. The Sanskrit term for these forces is *guna*, "rope," and the Gita explains how they pull us to act in various ways, even against our better judgment. These "ropes of influence" appear in three ways: *sattva* (goodness), *raja* (passion), and *tamas* (ignorance).

The effects of the *sattva-guna*, the mode of goodness, are seen when an atmosphere of peace, serenity, and harmony prevails in our environment and within our mind. The mode of passion or *raja-guna* rears its ugly head when we feel an overwhelming, insatiable desire for mortal things, striving for more, and when we feel persistently dissatisfied. *Tamo-guna*, the mode of ignorance, is indicated when a person feels lazy, depressed, or unmotivated and also when they are intoxicated or mentally unstable.

Srila Prabhupada believed that the most critical component for success in self-realization is to learn from great sages and saints who will "slacken the soul's attachment for matter." Thus a person can gradually rid themselves of the illusion of matter and false ego and be "promoted to the real life of eternity, knowledge and bliss."

In fact, association with such great souls is considered the "only auspicious activity" in this material world.

What I propose to do in this book is to pass on to you what I have learned from saintly mentors and present their wisdom in a palatable, pragmatic and non-sectarian manner.

The purpose of this book is two-fold:

1)   I would like you to embrace these 7 Maxims for Soul Happiness as a fundamental part of your new worldview;

2)   I want you to assert these truths in words and actions, through affirmation and exercising them in your relationships with others.

In other words, to get the most out of this book, you will have to put these 7 Maxims of Soul Happiness to the test, and I trust you will.

Maxim 1

The Human Body is a Blessing

"Everyone should consider his body as a priceless gift from one whom he loves above all, a marvellous work of art, of indescribable beauty, and mystery beyond human conception, and so delicate that a word, a breath, a look, nay, a thought may injure it."
– Nikola Tesla

The Material Energies

There are two ways of looking at this world we live in; one is to see it as just a random assortment of physical elements with no meaning behind the cause and effects we experience. One would thus conclude that we are a body that is born, eats, poops, gets sick, falls in love, grows old and eventually dies, becoming food for worms or ash.

The other way to view this world is through eyes anointed with devotion to an intelligent Designer, whose divine spiritual energies have expanded to accommodate souls having a physical experience in response to their desire to be independent Overlords. As a soul, this physical experience is offered as a sort of training ground for evolving our consciousness and providing us an opportunity to be the "master of our domain," until such time that we awaken to our true nature as interdependent souls created for the purpose of pure loving exchange and devotional servitude.

For the most part, we are all being programmed through education and society to embrace the first paradigm – to buckle down on studying the nature of this physical world without consideration for the essence, or spirit, that animates it.

According to the teachings of Krishna in the *Bhagavad-Gita*, this material world comprises eight gross and subtle energies: earth, water, fire, air, ether are the gross elements that make up everything we can experience with our senses, and then there are three subtle elements: mind, intelligence, and false ego. Each proceeding element is superior to the former. In other words, the false ego is more delicate and superior to the intelligence, and the intelligence is superior to the mind, and the mind is superior to the gross material elements.

Everything we experience in this mundane world is a combination of these eight elements.

The Superior Nature

Above these eight physical energies, however, is the superior spiritual energy of the soul. This superior energy is transcendental to the material senses; however, under the spell of illusion, misguided souls are trying to exploit the resources of these inferior material energies.

> Besides these, O mighty-armed Arjuna, there is another, superior energy of Mine, which comprises the living entities who are exploiting the resources of this material, inferior nature.[1]

Bhagavad-Gita scholar and guru, Srila Prabhupada comments:

> While exploiting the gross and subtle inferior energy (matter), the superior energy (the living entity)

---

[1] *Bhagavad-Gita As It Is*, verse 7.5 (BBT)

forgets his real spiritual mind and intelligence. This forgetfulness is due to the influence of matter upon the living entity. But when the living entity becomes free from the influence of the illusory material energy, he attains the stage called *mukti*, or liberation. The false ego, under the influence of material illusion, thinks, "I am matter, and material acquisitions are mine."

It is critical, therefore, that you understand your higher nature as a soul and that the real "you" that animates this material form has originated from the superior spiritual energy. Your material body is just a temporary vehicle to facilitate learning experiences and expression until such time that it becomes uninhabitable and you are forced to leave it and enter another material form according to your desire and karma.

You Get What You Desire And Deserve

The concept of karma is part of the ancient teachings of the *Bhagavad-Gita* but has now become common vernacular in modern culture, with musicians such as John Lennon singing songs like *Instant Karma*. The oversimplification of karma, however, with such comments like, "it is like the law of physics, for every action there is an equal and opposite reaction," have just led to the confusion surrounding it, with many wondering how on earth can a loving God allow bad things to happen to good people?

What we need to understand here is that karma is not an equal and opposite reaction. Instead, it is an extremely complex harmonizing mechanism of material nature with multiple layers of cause and effect. Let me explain with a fictitious scenario...

> Tommy decided one day to buy himself a new suit. He had done his research and found that the best place to buy it would be Chi Long's Discount Fashion store in downtown New York. He learned that the

owner, Mr. Chi Long offered special deals to the first customer on a full moon day.

Tomorrow just happened to be a full moon day, and so Tommy set the clock for 6 am so that he could catch the early morning express train and be at the store by 7:30 am. He surmised that the store opened at 8 am, so being 30 minutes early would be perfect.

As planned, Tommy was up bright and early at 6 am. He showered, dressed and took a quick breakfast before running to the bus stop to catch the train. Everything was going smoothly, until ten minutes into the ride the bus got a flat tire. Rather than wait for the driver to change it, Tommy raced out the bus and started running to the train station. The express train was leaving at 6:40. Tommy was panting heavily as he darted around other early morning commuters, each one focused on their destination for what looked like schools of fish moving every which way in unison.

Tommy arrived at the station at 6:35 am, just in time to catch the train but then scrambled to find the right change to purchase his ticket. He got in line at the ticket counter but each minute that went by seemed like an eternity. By the time Tommy reached the counter it was 6:39, he silently berated himself for not planning and purchasing a day pass yesterday. He finally got his ticket but missed the train. It was now 6:41. The next train would depart at 7:05. He could still make it before the store opened but now may not be the first customer.

As he waited for the next train, Tommy studied the other people at the station. One young woman looked European and was carrying a large red backpack. She looked exhausted and confused. Tommy approached her. "Hello, do you need some help?" The young lady's eyes lit up and replied, "Why, yes, if you don't mind?" "Sure," said Tommy, "how can I help you." "Well, I need to get downtown to catch a bus to Washington DC to see my dying grandmother, but I injured my back last night, and this backpack is nearly impossible for me to carry now. Could you help me carry it to the bus stop?" "Well, sure, but what station are you getting off? Tommy probed. "I get off at 33rd street," the young woman answered. "Hmm, well I need to get off at 14th street, so that is a bit early for me," said Tommy. "It's ok, I understand. Don't worry; I'll manage somehow," she offered back. "No, no, I insist," Tommy responded. "I think your business today is way more important than mine." "Oh, you are so kind. Thank you. It means a lot to me," she said sincerely. "May I ask, what is your business today?" she inquired. "Oh, nothing big, just that I wanted to purchase a new suit at this place where I could get a discount today," he said dismissively. "A new suit?" she responded with eagerness, as her eyebrows raised. "Yes, why?" "Well, it just so happens that my grandmother is the mother of Hugo Boss, the fashion icon," she said excitedly. "No, way," said Tommy." "Seriously?" "Yes, and I am sure I can help you get your new suit."

So you can see where this story goes. The point here is that along Tommy's journey that morning he had multiple decisions to make and each one of them led him down a specific karmic path that not only impacted him but every other person he encountered. And every other person that morning had to make just as many, if not more, decisions as they proceeded to their destination.

Every action, set in motion another chain of actions and in turn impacted, negatively or positively, another action in a veritable sea of actions and reactions. The young lady had her own story of how she happened to be standing at that particular spot on the train platform at that specific time when Tommy came down the stairs. And with hundreds of other people also on the platform, what was it that made her stand out in Tommy's scanning the crowd?

Furthermore, what prompted Tommy even to ask her if she needed help? Tommy would typically not do this, but that morning he felt compelled to do so. Why? Was there another 'player' involved? Who or what was prompting Tommy? Certainly, we could surmise that Tommy's decision that morning is a product of the thousands of other experiences he had had in the past. He had witnessed unconditional kindness. He had read about it, seen it in movies and so he knew how important it was. But why today? Why that mysterious girl on the platform?

You see, trying to formulate karma into a concise one-line statement is futile. The reality is, karma is Nature's urge to find balance while also fulfilling the desires of every one of us according to what we deserve at that particular time.

Most importantly, only if that thing we desired facilitated our life path and the life path of all those we had to interact with along the way. It's an incredibly complex system of justifying actions and reactions while serving to meet the individual needs of each participant. To suggest karma is anything but the work of a Supreme Intelligence is ludicrous.

What Is My Life Path?

Every birth we take has been designed to facilitate a particular life experience so that we can spiritually evolve. In other words, there is no such thing as evolution of species, there is only evolution of consciousness, with the various species we animate as souls, being vehicles for that spiritual evolution.

Whether we realize it or not, we did have a say in the parents we ended up with and this also is related to the kind of experience we desired to have in this current body.

Our life path or destiny is something that we either discover or waste years of our life denying. In numerology, the life path is described as our destiny number. We can understand what ours is by adding up the total number of our birthday. For example, my birthday is 4th November, 1963. So my total number is 4 + 1+1+1+9+6+3 = 25 (2+5) = 7.

But I am not just a destiny 7. I am a Day number 4 with a destiny 7. The combination of both the day and the total number is important in understanding the kind of 7 I am.

People that have a destiny of 7 can be philosophical if living positively, or have a victim mentality if living negatively. They are generally humanitarian, teachers, philosophers, and interested in mystical subjects; they enjoy serving and making sacrifices; they are "hands-on" people and prefer to learn by experience rather than being told what to do. They often struggle to practice what they preach to others. However, with my day number 4, I am inclined to the pragmatic side of the 7 path, leading to an interest in sports, health, and humanity and a unique ability to make the mystical understandable – distilling esoteric subjects and making them digestible, practical and believable.

Every number has its positive and debilitating qualities, and since both 4 and 7 are on the earth plane of the Numerology chart, a 4/7 living negatively, would be materialistic, miserly, and attached.

A major focus of my life thus far has been my work with my charity, Food for Life Global www.ffl.org whose mission is to teach spiritual equality through the unconditional act of liberally distributing plant-based meals that have been prepared with loving intention. An extension of this mission has been my book, *FOOD YOGA – Nourishing Body, Mind & Soul* which focused on demystifying the spiritual act of offering food to God and explaining how through developing a more respectful and devotional attitude towards food, anyone, regardless of their situation, can nourish their body, mind, and soul. Here again, we have the positive influence of 4 = health and wellness with 7 = mysticism and philosophy.

The bottom line here is that understanding your life path can be extremely helpful in guiding your life and career decisions. Sadly, too many people ignore the predictive sciences and prefer to just "go with the flow" like ships at sea without a rudder.

Knowing "what makes you tick" and what gets you excited is crucial for leading a successful life. And so I urge you to calculate your day and destiny numbers now and learn about the positive and debilitating qualities of each and what might be the most suitable life path for you. I will explain more about the quality of each number later in this book.

Human Life Is A Blessing

According to the 5000-year old Vedic scriptures of India, each soul migrates through millions of different life forms before reaching the human form. These same Vedic scriptures state that there are apparently 8.4 million different species of life on earth (mainstream science estimates 8.7 million[2]) and most souls will transmigrate through each and every kind of species before reaching the human form. Of course, there is no way to actually prove this. We just have to accept the fact that within each and every body a soul is present animating that life form and each one of them has their unique evolution story.

Someone has to be a pig; someone has to be a cockroach, yes? If we are to accept the notion that God is all good and fair, then it makes perfect sense that each and every one of us has transmigrated through each life form on our journey to enlightenment. You may find it very difficult to imagine yourself in the body of another species, but keep in mind that along with a physical form, the soul is given a certain mentality, intelligence, and consciousness that is perfectly suited for that particular physical form.

---

[2] About 8.7 million (give or take 1.3 million) is the new, estimated total number of species on Earth -- the most precise calculation ever offered -- with 6.5 million species on land and 2.2 million in oceans. Announced by the *Census of Marine Life*, the figure is based on a new analytical technique.

The human form is indeed a wonderful blessing as it is only in the human form that we can actually start to grasp the magnitude of life and the amazing opportunities afforded those in the human form.

According to the Vedas, it is in the human form that the soul has the capacity to understand the difference between spirit and matter and to investigate the mysteries of life itself. Whereas other life forms can experience happiness, peace and the joy of companionship, it is only in the human form that we can understand what these experiences mean and how each and every decision we make can either entangle us or free us from physical bondage.

We Are In The Minority

According to the latest statistics, as of this writing, there is an estimated 7.6 billion humans on earth. That seems like a lot but when you consider that according to The World Conservation Union, there are 1.73 million other species, and when you multiply the actual number within each species, humans are really just a tiny portion of the incredibly diverse earth plane we all live on.

Then of course, there is the spiritual realm.

"How can we measure those numbers?" you might ask. We can't, but what we can do is accept what the great sages and saints have described in the various spiritual literatures of the world, and that is, that the spiritual realm is where the majority of life exists. According to the Vedas, the entire material creation is like a small dark cloud in the spiritual sky. In other words, every living being, sky scrapper, city, country, planet, galaxy and universe within this material creation is but a small cloud in the entire spiritual sky.

Perspective like this can be a real buzz kill. When we stop to think about it, that tiny ant that is moving across the floor of your apartment is no less significant than us humans going about our daily affairs. For the ant, your footsteps will appear to be like thunder and your shadow like a dark cloud covering the sun. In the same way, from the perspective of higher beings, humans going about their business are no more significant than an ant.

As long as we fail to recognize the tremendous advantage and spiritual opportunity we have as humans, we will never achieve spiritual fulfilment.

The Amazing Human Machine

The human body is an absolute marvel of creation.

In an article titled *"Dissecting Darwinism,"* Doctor Joseph Kuhn of the Baylor University Medical Center pointed out serious flaws in Darwinian evolution by asserting that life could not possibly have come from chemicals, since DNA code absolutely required input from outside of nature.

He then addressed Darwinism's failure to account for the uncompromising architecture of cellular systems, especially within the human form. As a medical doctor, Kuhn understands the interdependent nature of biochemical systems that preserve and regulate all parts of the body, and that the human body contains an inflexible system in which its essential parts and biochemicals **must exist all at once** for the body to function, which challenges any notion of a single cell organisms mutating into more complex life forms.

Another biochemist, Michael Behe called these uncompromising architectures of cellular systems "irreducibly complex." In other words, removing a single core part from one of these systems stops the entire system from working, thus confirming that each system was initially built with all of its parts intact. "There is no way that these systems could have evolved over time. They were perfectly structured from the beginning," he suggests.

This is exactly what Creationist would expect to see, rather than nature accidentally constructing living systems bit-by-bit over vast stretches of time—as Darwinian proponents maintain.

Kuhn cited the work of another medical doctor, Geoffrey Simmons, who pointed out that these interdependent biochemical systems also require regulation. For example, just as a person would die without their heart, they would also die without the vital blood biochemical haemoglobin. Similarly, a heart that beats too fast or too slow would be just as lethal as having no heart at all, and a body that produces too much or too little haemoglobin would be equally lethal. Thus, the systems that regulate haemoglobin and heartbeats must also have been present from the beginning.

Virtually every aspect of human physiology has regulatory elements, developmental components and feedback loops that require the service of thousands of interacting genes. Thus, Kuhn asserts, "the human body represents an irreducibly complex system on a cellular and an organ/system basis."

Darwin's evolution theory has no proven explanation for the origin of just one irreducibly complex system, what to speak of the millions interdependent networks of irreducible systems that comprise the human body.

According to Kuhn, to transform another creature into a human "would require far more than could be expected from random mutation and natural selection." However, a perfectly constructed, self-regulating life form is exactly what an all-wise divine Creator would make.

DNA Instructions

For most people, DNA is a mystery and something that is discussed solely in the laboratory by biologists or forensic scientists or a long forgotten topic they learned about in high school. However, DNA is something we should all understand, for the simple reason that DNA, and specifically the genetic code that manages your DNA, has a major influence on the kind of person you are and the opportunities you are afforded in life. Let me explain…

DNA instructions or the genetic code that manages your DNA are extremely complex in nature. It is estimated that it would take something like 100 pages of DNA instructions to manage just one cell in your body! The human body has an estimated 37.2 trillion cells so the genetic code to program all the cells in just one human body is beyond astronomical and clearly points to the fingerprint of a divine Creator.

DNA is theorized as a kind of micro supercomputer as it has to re-create the entire human genome within the very first mother cell, which means every cell mitosis isn't exactly the same but is ordained chronologically to complete the stages of cell life before life begins as a baby. Indeed, even the sperm cell has a kind of consciousness to enable it to compete with other sperms to find the egg of the mother. All cell nucleuses have their own consciousness with preordained DNA codes intact. The strangest mystery is why the 37.2 trillion cells that make up a human body die off once the human body expires. It's as if the soul that was formerly hosting that body ("the landlord," if you will) has left the premises and so by occupation law, all the "residents" of that body (cells) have to evacuate and be transferred to a new building (another life form).

Each cell is animated by a soul and so this transmigration is no different than the soul of a human reincarnating to another human or animal form, based on their karma and desire. In the case of cells, however, it is purely a karmic play as the soul evolves in awareness taking on different forms.

How Many Cells Are In Your Body?

Each cell has a life span of from a few days to a lifetime. While red blood cells live for about four months, white blood cells live on average more than a year. Skin cells live about two to three weeks, while colon cells die off after about four days. Sperm cells have a life span of only about three days, while brain cells typically last an entire lifetime.

As each cell dies, they are being replaced by a new cell fully-loaded with its own set of specific DNA instructions for that functioning of that cell, as well as the entire genome of the body.

Most human cells carry 2 copies of the genome and are known as diploid cells. One copy comes from each of your parents, so they aren't identical, but similar. However, sperm and egg cells only carry one copy of the genome and are known as haploid cells. During fertilization the 2 cells merge their copies and make a diploid zygote. At the chromosomal level, humans have 23 chromosomes, so a diploid cell has 2 copies of each so a total of 46 chromosomes.

As the body matures, cells are dying off and being replaced all the time, so it's not clear where the popular myth began that cells are renewed every seven years. I remember hearing this when I was a monk as many of my teachers would claim as such to prove how the body is changing while the soul remains constant. I just accepted this as a fact but it turns out the cell lifecycle is much more variegated.

Naturally, cells cannot communicate to us to help us unravel this mystery. Certainly we can look through a microscope and count off the number of cells in particular organs but this method is far from practical. While some types of cells are easy to spot, others weave themselves up into obscurity. Even if you could count ten cells each second, it would take you tens of thousands of years to finish counting the number of cells in one human body, what to speak of the challenge of chopping a body up into tiny patches for microscopic viewing.

The closest estimate for the total number of cells in a human body came from a study published in *Annals of Human Biology*, entitled rather appropriately, *"An Estimation of the Number of Cells in the Human Body."*

The authors – a team of scientists from Italy, Greece, and Spain looked back over scientific journals and books from the past two centuries and found many estimates that presented a huge disparity, from 5 billion to 200 million trillion cells. What was more surprising was that none of these previous reports offered an explanation for how they came up with the estimate. It was all just conjecture and yet these were official scientific journals!

If it's not feasibly possible to count all the cells in a human body, how can scientists estimate the total? One method proposed is to take the average weight of a cell, which is approximately 1 nanogram and multiply that by body weight. For the average adult man weighing 70 kilograms, a simple calculation would lead us to conclude that his body is made up of about 70 trillion cells.

It's also possible to make an estimation based on the volume of cells. So if we take for example the average volume of a mammal cell, estimated at 4 billionth of a cubic centimetre, then we would conclude that this same 70kg male contains 15 trillion cells. Now that's quite a disparity but what makes matters worse is that the cells that pack our bodies are not lined up in a uniform way. Cells come in different sizes and densities. If, for example, you used the density of red blood cells to estimate the total, your total number would be even higher – a staggering 724 trillion cells – because red blood cells are packed very tightly. Skin cells, on the other hand, are so spread out that they'd give you a measly total of just 35 billion cells.

So the authors of the above mentioned paper set out to calculate the number of cells in the body by breaking it down by organs and cell types. They tallied the volume and density of cells in the intestines, gallbladders, liver, joints, and bone marrow, etc., and then came up with estimates for the total number of each kind of cell. For example, they estimated that we have just 2 billion heart muscle cells and 50 billion fat cells. By adding up all the numbers they arrived at 37.2 trillion cells.

Whether the actual number is 37.2 trillion or 200 trillion, both numbers are astronomical and should help us appreciate just how complex this human body is. If, as I mentioned earlier, it requires something like 100 pages of genetic code to instruct just one cell in our body to perform its particular function, then we're talking about a genetic instruction manual for the entire human body of 37.2 trillion x 100 or 37,200,000,000,000,000 printed pages of text, or a book that would scale to 2,201,704,545 miles high! Another way to visualize this is that this distance would cover 3 visits to Jupiter and back. And so the fact that Darwinian philosophers and scientists have the audacity to suggest that the human body evolved through random events is utterly absurd.

Super Human Powers

The human body has its limits but often those limits are created by our minds. The fact is, the bar for "human limits" is being raised all the time. Just think of the Olympics of the early 20th century compared to today's Olympics. The same applies to every sporting event on the planet. Human capacity and abilities are constantly improving. However, there are times when even non-athletic people excel way beyond their normal physical abilities when under extreme stress. For example, a father pulling off a car door to save his child from burning. So what makes this happen? What is that thing that seemingly turns ordinary people into super humans?

That something is the body's fear response. When people find themselves under intense pressure, say for example a high-level competition or an emergency, the mental creation of fear unleashes reserves of energy that normally remain inaccessible. Granted, everyone feels and reacts to fear differently, for it is the seed of our fight or flight response. In those cases, where a person chooses to fight, they can often become superhuman in their response.

This acute stress response of the body is triggered by the body's sympathetic nervous system which releases hormones to help a person deal with a threat full on or to flee to safety.

The adrenal gland dumps cortisol and adrenaline into the blood stream. Blood pressure surges and the heart races, delivering oxygen and energy to the muscles. It's the biological equivalent of slamming your foot on the gas pedal and pushing extra fuel through the carburettor.

After the threat is gone, it can take between 20 to 60 minutes for the body to return to its pre-arousal levels.

Vladimir Zatsiorsky, a professor of kinesiology at Penn State suggests that there is a huge difference between the force that our muscles are able to theoretically apply, which he calls "absolute strength," and the maximum force that they can generate through the conscious exertion of will, which he calls "maximal strength." For example, an ordinary person, might be able to summon about 65 percent of their absolute power in a training session, while a trained weightlifter can exceed 80 percent and even higher when under extreme competitive conditions like the Olympics or the *World's Strongest Man* events, which he describes as "competitive maximum strength." It's important to note that these parameters are not fixed numbers—the more intense the competition, the higher the numbers can go, as the brain's fear response increasingly eliminates any limitation against performance.

In fact, these "super human levels" are somewhat contagious in high level sporting events. When Michael Phelps won the 100-meter butterfly in 50.58 seconds at the 2008 Olympics, breaking the previous Olympic record, three of the other seven swimmers who finished after him also came in ahead of the previous record.

But there's a limit to how fast and how strong fear can make us. Zatsiorsky's work suggests that while fear can indeed stimulate someone to approach their absolute power levels, there's no way they will exceed it. A woman who can lift 100 pounds at the gym might be able to lift 135 pounds in a frenzy of maternal fear, suggests Zatsiorsky, but she's never going to be able to lift a 3,000-pound car off of a trapped child.

The mechanisms by which the body is able to summon greater reserves of power are still under investigation, but many believe it may be related to analgesia, or the body's ability to temporarily shut down pain and thus be able to push beyond our usual limits. When you're at the gym, straining to complete the last rep of an exercise, it's hard to imagine your muscles having the capacity to work any harder than they already are as your body's production of lactic acid goes into overdrive, releasing an excess of hydrogen ions into your muscles. When there is an excessive build-up of these ions it inhibits muscle contraction which then leads to the burning sensation we all experience.

But under intense pressure—whether it's an Olympic competition, a child trapped inside a burning car, or an attacking dog—we experience a total absence of pain without loss of consciousness and are able to do seemingly superhuman things that are impossible to replicate afterwards.

What Is Consciousness?

The world of consciousness research is big business. The currently accepted definition[3] of consciousness is:

> "the state of being aware of oneself and the environment. It is associated with wakefulness, responsiveness and arousal. Consciousness is typically measured by verbal reports about experience. Related areas of interest are those functions that are thought to operate without consciousness, such as blind sight and subliminal perception.

As you can see, for mainstream science, consciousness is still looked upon as something that results from a unique set of physical circumstances and elements.

However, scientists all over the world have had to rethink what consciousness is from a biological perspective, when it was revealed in a research page published on *The Lancet*[4] that a French man had lived a relatively normal, healthy life - despite having lost 90 percent of his brain!

Most scientists believe that the physical source of consciousness is found in the brain, but this man's example begged the questions: how can he be lacking the majority of his neurons and yet still be aware of himself and his surroundings? What is more amazing is that he did not realize he had any neurological damage until the time of the examinations back in 2007 when he visited the

---

[3] Definition of consciousness taken from Nature.com
[4] See: http://bit.ly/2PYssAL

doctor complaining of mild weakness in his left leg. Later, brain scans revealed that his skull was mostly filled with fluid, leaving just a thin outer layer of actual brain tissue. The majority of the man's brain had slowly eroded away over the course of 30 years by the build-up of fluid in the brain, a condition known as hydrocephalus that he had been diagnosed with as a child.

But despite his condition, the man wasn't mentally disabled, although he had a low IQ of 75, he was working happily as a civil servant and was married with two children.

Examples like this challenge our understanding of consciousness. "Any theory of consciousness has to be able to explain why a person like that, who's missing 90 percent of his neurons, still exhibits normal behaviour," asked Axel Cleeremans, a cognitive psychologist from the Université Libre de Bruxelles in Belgium.

However, Cleeremans and other scientists studying this case are sticking to their guns and claiming that even though the man's remaining brain was only tiny, the neurons left over were able to still generate a theory about themselves, which means the man remained conscious of his actions.

According to the Vedas, however, consciousness is a symptom of the presence of a soul and rather than being a condition borne out of material circumstances, it is the innate quality of the soul which is having to filter its experience through layers of mental conditioning, false ego and processing that experience through the medium of a brain.

Granted, this man's capacity to understand his experience was limited and this is confirmed by his low IQ, however, he was conscious and fully aware of his material identity and interactions.

As the soul transmigrates through different bodies it must contend with a certain set of senses and mental conditioning suited to that physical form. However, once the soul enters a human form, it has the most perfect set of circumstances and mentality for self-realization, simply because the human form is the closest facsimile to our original spiritual form.

In Genesis 1:26 it is stated: "Let us make man in our image, **in our likeness**."[5] Accordingly, humanity is unique among all God's creations.

The Gift Of The Human Form

Our senses are inferior in their knowledge-acquiring capacity compared to animals and insects and yet we have the greatest opportunity for spiritual advancement. How so?

Only in the human form do we have the ability to understand the true nature of this material world and to question our existence.

Furthermore, only in the human form can we understand the nature of suffering and the lessons contained within those experiences. If our sole focus in life is to enjoy there are far better life forms to facilitate that, whereas in the human form we have to undergo all kinds of suffering to enjoy even the most basic pleasurable experiences. Take for example, eating, whereas an animal like a cow can happily chew on grass, a human must either work to earn money to pay for food or make the effort to till the field and grow food from seed to plant. Then there is the example of sex, whereas a male human must go through various mating rituals, and often spend lots of money to court his desired mate, a pigeon will happily have sex up to 50-times a day with multiple partners! Similarly, whereas we humans must comply with taxation, incur debt to acquire a home, etc., an animal will happily sleep under a tree. In more ways than one, we can clearly see that the human species is challenged just to make ends meet, which lends credence to the claim of saints and sages that human life is not meant solely for sensual enjoyment but rather for self-realization so that one can escape the bonds of a physical form altogether.

Consider the fact that there are 4 fundamental activities of every animal – eating, sleeping, mating, and defending.

---

[5] New International Version (NIV)

If as humans, we do not strive for more than this than what distinguishes us from other animals?

The gift of human birth is one of the three blessings of life. There are innumerable life forms in the creation but only a small minority are humans. Sadly, however, the majority of humans lead an animal existence and are asleep to the full potential of their humanity, sleepwalking through their daily lives mechanically until they chance upon a saint who implores them to awaken! The second blessing of human life is when the desire for liberation from physical bondage takes root in a person after they wake up to the fact of their spiritual nature. The third gift is the opportunity to come under the grace of a saint and evolve spiritually under their guidance.

The most natural way to cultivate this higher awareness is through meditation and acts of unconditional service to others. It is by such acts that one's consciousness is naturally shifted to the higher frequency of soul, wherein one begins to see the spiritual equality and interdependence of all beings.

Of course, history has shown that humans have used various herbs and medicinal plants, like psilocybin mushrooms, peyote and the vine leaves that make up *Ayahuasca*, a traditional indigenous drink of the Amazonian and Andean peoples of South America, to also expand their consciousness. However, it should be noted that all of these hallucinogenic experiences last but a few hours and only serve to inspire people to change their perspective on life. Eventually, one has to do the manual work of expanding their consciousness and living to the full potential of their higher self in order to escape the bondage of rebirth.

All of these things are uniquely human and to miss out on this opportunity would be the greatest travesty.

AFFIRMATION 1

I am an eternal spirit soul and my human form is a blessing that has been gifted to me. I value and cherish the amazing opportunity this human form affords me for self-realization.

Maxim 2

Death is Nothing to Fear

"I existed from all eternity and, behold, I am here; and I shall exist till the end of time, for my being has no end."
- Khalil Gibran

The Soul Just Moves On

As energetic beings, we can never cease to be, for energy is eternal and just changes shape. What was one physical form, becomes something else over time. A seed becomes a tree; a tree becomes a table; a table become fire wood and that fire then turns the wood to ashes, which in turn becomes soil and later that soil, rich with minerals, makes up the body of a new plant. While all this transmutation is taking place, there is one constant – the soul is present through every change. Indeed, wherever there is life, symptomized by consciousness and growth, there is the presence of a soul. So if the soul is eternal why do we fear death?

We fear death for a few reasons:

1. We misidentify our true self with the temporary physical form it currently animates.
2. We assume there is nothing after death
3. We are told that we will burn in hell for our sins
4. We think that death is painful

Let's address these challenges one by one.

We've already established the fact there is something superior that animates the physical body that is the source of life – the soul – the true self that is bewildered by illusion. However, even though you may intellectually grasp this, the fact remains that you and I are conditioned to think otherwise, through generations of past programming that has literally rewritten our genetic code and decades of current programming from peers, family, and the media. So overcoming this fear requires more than just a mental adjustment. It requires hard work – purifying our minds, practicing detachment and reprogramming our perception of this world.

To think that there is nothing after death, is both foolish and illogical. For one thing, every day we see how death leads to renewal – old decomposed fruits and vegetables become the source of life for new fruits and vegetables in the form of composted soil. It is foolish too, because we inherently feel eternal, which is our nature as a soul, and no matter how hard we try, we cannot grasp the finality of death. Even the most ignorant people will speak of relatives and friends that have died, by saying "*they* have passed on." Or "*they* are now looking down on us," etc. In other words, we all inherently believe there is a life after death.

Hard line Christianity, or the "Fire and brimstone" form, is famous for espousing the belief that sinners will literally burn in hell. I think I speak for most people when I say that this idea is utterly ridiculous and certainly not consistent with the concept of a fair and loving God. If God, by definition is fair and loving, then why would He/She ever consider that allowing someone to burn in hell indefinitely was a reasonable punishment? It is absurd and anyone with half a brain knows that such tactics are used by religious zealots to enslave their followers to the church or temple.

The idea is illogical too, for how does a soul eternally burn in hell, when by definition, souls are of the superior energy, god-like, and transcendental to anything mundane and hellish.

The Vedic literatures, specifically the *Srimad Bhagavatam* sheds some light on this topic. It is explained in the 5th Canto that those souls that commit sinful acts in their human form, will have to suffer for their sins in the next physical form, as played out according to the law of karma. For example, a man that has a gluttonous and indiscriminate appetite will most likely take birth as a pig where he can better fulfil his gluttonous desires. Krishna in the *Bhagavad-Gita* explains:

> The living entity, thus taking another gross body, obtains a certain type of ear, eye, tongue, nose and sense of touch, which are grouped about the mind. He thus enjoys a particular set of sense objects.[6]

However, before this soul transmigrates to that pig form, he/she will also have to suffer in the astral realm for all the animals they had killed. This punishment on the astral plane may indeed feel like an eternity but in fact is mere moments of time in human time scales, just like a dream experience, that may seem like years but in reality is just a few minutes of elapsed time in the physical realm.

The astral body that carries our soul from one body to the next plays an important role in preparing us and facilitating our desires. I will explain more on this topic later.

Finally, we may be scared of death because we fear we will suffer, when in reality, to die just means the soul is forced to leave a particular physical form because that body has become uninhabitable. For most souls, death is nothing more than leaving one room to enter another, or as Krishna explains in the *Bhagavad-Gita*:

> As a person puts on new garments, giving up old ones, the soul similarly accepts new material bodies, giving up the old and useless ones[7].

---

[6] *Bhagavad-Gita As It Is*, verse 15.9 (BBT)
[7] *Bhagavad-gita As It Is*, verse 2.22 (BBT)

However, for those souls that have built up extreme attachment through years of cultivating a false identification with a physical body, death can be excruciatingly difficult, as they are unceremoniously yanked from their false reality to some unknown place. Certainly, if one dies of a chronic illness like cancer, then the preceding months before death can be overwhelmingly painful, however, the actual passing of the soul from one body to another is at least not physically painful. The so-called "pain" experienced by conditioned souls at death is entirely mental and results from attachment to the body. The soul is always transcendental but due to the influence of a false ego, we identify with a body and therefore think we are suffering when in reality it is akin to a driver feeling "pain" in seeing his car damaged from an accident.

The Only Thing You Can Take With You Is Your Wisdom

This material world is transient by nature – we pretend to be this or that; we assume we own this or that; we believe we belong to this or that social group, etc., when in fact, nothing is permanent. India's *Srimad Bhagavatam* talks about this material world as the "World of names," wherein we artificially give something a sense of permanence by giving it a name, when in fact, as George Harrison once sang, *"All things must pass."*

We enter this world naked and often nameless, and we will leave this world bereft of all material possessions. All we can really take with us is the accumulated wisdom (self-awareness) and the karmic credit or debit resulting from our pious or impious actions. This "credit" or "debit" manifests in the kind of body we are next given, the family we are born into, the place, time and circumstances we are presented; and the skills, fortune, and intelligence or lack thereof, etc., we are afforded.

Annie Besant[8] once wrote:

---

[8] (1847 – 1933) A British socialist, theosophist, women's rights activist, writer, orator, and supporter of both Irish and Indian self-rule.

"The soul grows by reincarnation in bodies provided by nature, more complex, more powerful, as the soul unfolds greater and greater faculties. And so the soul climbs upward into the light eternal. And there is no fear for any child of man, for inevitably **he climbs towards God."**

And this is the beauty of life itself – that we are always making progress – no matter what our current circumstances may dictate.

The perfection of human life therefore is to learn as much about your higher self as you can in each human incarnation. How you go about that is uniquely yours. This is your life and you are the one experiencing it, not someone else. So do not fall into the self-deprecating trap of living your life according to the demands of someone else. Of course, there is a time in all our lives where we must submit to a superior teacher for bettering ourselves, but at a certain point in time, one must "fly their own plane", or "leave the nest" and find their way in life according to one's unique set of skills and passion. We ourselves must become a teacher of souls and share the wisdom.

As we strive toward our dreams, lessons will naturally come our way and so it behoves us to embrace those lessons and evolve and not remain stubborn, static and irrelevant. Change has to be welcomed for nothing in this world remains the same.

Living In The Moment

This world is considered "fleeting," specifically because time is the ultimate controller and time by nature is elusive. It never sits still; it never persists; it is always in motion. What we can extract from this elusive quality of time is the fact that living with full attention **in the moment** is the closest we will ever get to a sense of eternality, as long as we are embodied.

Our life is a garland of now moments strung together on an invisible thread called time. Each one of us has a unique "garland" made up of things we experienced ("ornaments") in this life. Magically, however, each one of those "ornaments" on this garland fades away the instant our focus is removed from them and is immediately replaced by yet another "ornament." Paradoxically, the garland itself is illusory and yet the "ornaments" are real, at least for that moment we focused on them.

Our life unfolds in the present. But so often, like water, we allow the present to slip through our fingers while we gaze at our reflection. When we allow moments in our life to be squandered away unobserved and unappreciated and worry about the elusive future or lament about the past, we commit the greatest disservice to the human condition. Sadly, our modern lives are filled with an overwhelming array of distractions, and as a result, we rarely stop to breathe and contemplate.

While at work, our tendency is to fantasize about being on vacation and then when we finally go on vacation, we fear about the work piling up on our desks! We dwell on unpleasant memories of the past and agonize about what may or may not have happened then and what may or may not happen in the future. We fail to appreciate living in the present because our minds are so agitated and uncontrolled, like a monkey in a marketplace.

Most of us seldom take time out for contemplation but spend most of our time chasing fleeting memories or unattainable desires.

"Ordinary thoughts course through our mind like a deafening waterfall," wrote Jon Kabat-Zinn, the biomedical scientist who introduced meditation into mainstream medicine. In order to gain control of our "waterfall-like" minds, we need to step outside of the flow, to pause, and stop doing, and just focus on being.

Living in the moment—also called mindfulness—is a state of intentionally focusing on the present. When you are mindful, you tap into your higher self and realize that your thoughts are not you but are just expressions of the mind energy – one of the eight energies that make up our material experience. We need to become observers of our thoughts – "a witness" if you will – from moment to moment without judging them.

Mindfulness or introspection involves being fully aware of

your thoughts and yet detached – neither grasping at them nor pushing them away. Instead of allowing your life to pass you by frivolously, you awaken to the full life experience.

Cultivating a non-judgmental and detached awareness of the present bestows a host of benefits. Mindfulness can reduce stress, boost the immune system, reduce chronic pain, lower blood pressure, and can even help patients suffering with chronic disease like cancer. By spending even a few minutes of the day actively focusing on living in the moment you can dramatically reduce the risk of heart disease.

For example, the mind-calming practice of meditation may play a role in reducing your risk of heart disease, according to a scientific statement published in the Sept. 28, 2017, *Journal of the American Heart Association.*[9]

"Not only can meditation improve how your heart functions, but a regular practice can enhance your outlook on life and motivate you to maintain many heart-healthy behaviours, like following a proper diet, getting adequate sleep, and keeping up regular exercise," says Dr. John Denninger, director of research at the Harvard-affiliated Benson-Henry Institute for Mind Body Medicine at Massachusetts General Hospital.

Mindful people are more relaxed, happier, empathetic, conscientious and feel a greater sense of security. They have higher self-esteem and are more accommodating with those that challenge their worldview and are typically less defensive. By anchoring your awareness in the here and now you can avoid all kinds of impulsive behaviour that typically underlies depression, binge eating, and attention deficit.

How To Prepare For The Last Breath

Death is the final curtain for the soul's experience in a particular body; however, it is not the final curtain on life itself, for the soul

---

[9] Source: *Harvard Health Publishing, Harvard Medical School.* http://bit.ly/2N0sW7m

"is unborn, eternal, ever-existing, undying and primeval," says Krishna in the *Bhagavad-Gita* verse 2.20.

For most people, death is something to fear but for the enlightened soul, death is the inevitable changing of the material condition and the gateway for a new beginning.

The *Bhagavad-Gita* Verse 2:69 declares:

> *What is night for all beings is the time of awakening for the self-controlled; and the time of awakening for all beings is night for the introspective sage.*

Vedic scholar, Srila Prabhupada comments: "Activities of the introspective sage, or thoughtful man, are night for persons materially absorbed. Materialistic persons remain asleep in such a night due to their ignorance of self-realization."

The fact is that death is the ultimate testing ground for our self-realization. If we've put in the time and done the work of cultivating awareness of our higher self, we'll be more than ready for death's calling. If, however, we have spent our life cultivating attachment to worldly things and pandering to our external identity, death will be a most unwelcome guest, and most certainly very frightening.

Ask any nurse that has worked in the terminally ill ward how scared most people are as death approaches. I remember doing just that when I first started asking questions about death and was told the following story by one Nurse Judy who worked at the Paddington Royal Women's Hospital in Sydney.

> "I remember one night, one elderly man called Charles started calling out to us in the nurse's station, "help me, they are coming for me, help!" We immediately ran into his room only to find him looking around the room in total anxiety and fear. Charles was obviously seeing something that we could not. Our presence, however, seemed to have a calming effect on him and he relaxed. But the next night he died of a heart attack."

How A Sinful Man Was Saved At The Last Moment

So what exactly happened to Charles?

We can get some insight from the story of Ajamila as described in the *Bhagavat Purana* of India.

Ajamila, who was considered a greatly sinful man, was miraculously liberated when four order carriers of Lord Vishnu came to rescue him from the hands of the order carriers of Yamaraja (the Lord of Death).

Sinful activities are painful both in this life and in the next. We should know for certain that the cause of all suffering in life is due to immoral behaviour. In performing our day-to-day work, inevitably we cause suffering to other living beings, even in the benign act of gathering of food, hundreds of insects are harmed, and therefore, according to the guidelines set forth by the Vedic scriptures, different types of atonement are recommended to counteract the sinful activity we even perform unknowingly.

However, the various methods of atonement (austerity, penance, celibacy, control of the mind and senses, truthfulness and the practice of mystic yoga, etc.,) do not necessarily free a person from ignorance, which is the root of all immoral behaviour. None of these methods can free one from the tendency to commit immoral acts again.

As the story of Ajāmila will illustrate, through the practice of bhakti-yoga (devotional service) one can thoroughly cleanse the heart and mind of the tendency for immoral life, but even if one happens to deviate they can be saved from sinful reaction by restarting their devotional practice, even if unknowingly. The story was narrated by the great sage, Śukadeva Gosvāmī to King Parīkṣit and appears in the *Srimad Bhagavatam* 6 canto, chapters 1 and 2 starting at verse 21. I have edited the story for brevity and clarity.

> In the city known as Kānyakubja in India, there was a brāhmaṇa named Ajāmila who while collecting flowers in the field for worshipping the Lord, he happened to see a drunken man and a prostitute

engaged in sex. Although he tried hard to forget what he saw, Ajāmila became bewildered and attracted to the prostitute.

Although Ajāmila was a strict brāhmaṇa, he foolishly took this prostitute into his home as a maidservant. Inevitably, he became so entangled that he abandoned his family, wife, and children and went off with the prostitute. Due to his illicit connection with the prostitute, he lost all his good qualities, completely forgot his values, and indulged in sinful life.

The disgraced brāhmaṇa then earned his livelihood and maintained his prostitute wife and children by cheating in gambling or by directly stealing from others.

While he thus spent his time in abominable activities to maintain his large family of ten sons, eighty-eight years of his life passed.

Due to his past spiritual upbringing, however, Ajāmila fortuitously named his youngest son Nārāyaṇa[10], which happened to be one of the many holy names of Vishnu (God).

Because of the child's broken language and awkward movements, Ajāmila was attached to the boy and enjoyed the child's company. When Ajāmila took his meals or drank, he called the child to eat or drink with him.

Being fully occupied in taking care of the child and calling the boy's name, Nārāyaṇa, Ajāmila was unaware that his own life was now exhausted and that death was upon him.

---

[10] The Bhagavata Purana and Veda declares Narayana as a part of the Trimurti who creates unlimited universes and enters each one of them.

When the time of death arrived for Ajāmila, he began thinking exclusively of his son Nārāyaṇa.

At that moment, Ajāmila saw three hideous and fierce-looking persons with deformed bodily features, twisted faces, and hair standing erect on their bodies at the foot of his bed. With ropes in their hands, they had come to take him away to the abode of Yamarāja[11], the Lord of Death. Upon seeing these ugly creatures, Ajāmila was extremely bewildered and began calling his son loudly by his name. Thus with tears in his eyes, he unintentionally chanted the holy name of Nārāyaṇa.

The Vishnudūtas immediately arrived when they heard the holy name of their master from the mouth of the dying Ajāmila, who had called out without offense because he had chanted in complete anxiety.

The ugly servants of Yamarāja, known as the Yamadūtas, were just about to snatch the soul from the core of the heart of Ajāmila, but with booming voices the Vishnudūtas forbade them to do so.

When the Yamadūtas were thus forbidden, they replied: "Who are you, that you dare to challenge the jurisdiction of Yamarāja, the son of the Sun God? Where have you come from and why are you forbidding us to touch the body of Ajāmila? Your eyes are just like the petals of lotus flowers. Dressed in yellow silken garments, decorated with garlands of lotuses, and wearing beautiful helmets on your heads and earrings on your ears, you all appear fresh and youthful. Your long arms are decorated

---

[11] **Yamarāja** is a god of death, the south direction, and the underworld, [1] belonging to an early stratum of Rigvedic Hindu deities. In Christian theology, Yamaraja is akin to the Judge. See: https://en.wikipedia.org/wiki/Yama

with bows and quivers of arrows and with swords, clubs, conch shells, discs and lotus flowers. Your effulgence has dissipated the darkness of this place with amazing illumination. So please tell us, why are you obstructing us?"

Being thus addressed by the messengers of Yamarāja, the servants of Vishnu smiled and spoke the following words in voices as deep as the sound of rumbling clouds.

"If you are servants of Yamarāja, you must explain to us the process of punishing others? Who are the actual candidates for punishment?"

The Yamadūtas replied:

"The Supreme Lord Nārāyaṇa is situated in the spiritual world, but He controls the entire cosmic manifestation. In this way, all living entities are awarded different qualities, different social positions, various duties, and different forms according to their karma.

"The sun, fire, sky, air, demigods, moon, evening, day, night, directions, water, land and the Lord within the heart all witness the activities of every living being.

"The candidates for punishment are those who are confirmed by these many witnesses to have deviated and sinned. No one, therefore, is immune to being subjected to punishment because of their sinful acts.

"O Vishnudūtas, while you are sinless, those within this material world are not, whether acting piously or impiously, because one who has accepted a material body cannot be inactive, and therefore, sinful action

34

is inevitable. All the living being within this material world are punishable.

"In proportion to the extent of one's sinful or pious actions in this life, one must enjoy or suffer the corresponding reactions of their karma in the next.

"We can see three different varieties of life, those that are peaceful and those that are restless or foolish. Each of them can be understood as happy, unhappy or in-between; or as religious, irreligious and semireligious. We can deduce that in the next life these three kinds of natures will similarly act.

"Just as springtime in the present indicates the nature of spring in the past and future, so this life of happiness, distress or a mixture of both gives evidence concerning the pious and impious activities of one's past and future lives.

"The omnipotent Yamarāja can mentally observe the past activities of a particular soul and understand how they will act in future lives.

"As a sleeping person acts according to the body manifested in his dreams and accepts it to be himself, so one identifies with his present body, which he acquired because of his past pious or impious actions, and is unable to know his past or future lives.

"Above the five senses of perception, the five working senses and the five objects of the senses is the mind, which is the sixteenth element. Above the mind is the seventeenth element, the soul, the living being himself, who, in cooperation with the other sixteen, enjoys the material world alone. The soul enjoys three kinds of situations, namely happy, distressful and mixed.

"The subtle body is composed of insurmountably strong desires, and therefore it causes the living entity to transmigrate from one body to another in human life, animal life and life as a demigod. When the living entity gets the body of a demigod, he is undoubtedly very jubilant, when he gets a human body he is always in lamentation, and when he gets the body of an animal, he is always afraid. In all conditions, however, the soul is miserable for having to transmigrate from one body to the next perpetually.

"The foolish embodied soul, hopeless at controlling his mind and senses, is forced to act according to the influence of material nature, like a silkworm that uses its saliva to create a cocoon that then becomes trapped in it. The bewildered soul traps themselves in a network of fruitive activities and has no way to escape.

"Not a single living being can remain unengaged even for a moment. One must act by their natural tendency which forcibly makes the soul work in a particular way.

"The fruitive actions a living being performs, whether pious or impious, are the unseen cause for the fulfillment of their desires and the deciding factor for the soul's different bodies. Because of their intense passion, the soul takes birth in a particular family and receives a body which is either like that of their mother or father.

"However, if in the human form of life, a soul is taught how to associate with and serve the Supreme Personality of Godhead or His devotee, their frustrating predicament can be overcome."

Saved By The Holy Name

The Vishnudūtas replied: "How painful it is that irreligion is being introduced into an assembly where religion should be maintained and a sinless person is about to be punished.

"Ajāmila has already atoned for sins performed in millions of lives, for in a helpless condition he chanted the holy name of God. Even though he did not do so purely, just by chanting the holy name of God without offense, he has sufficiently atoned for the sinful reactions of millions of lives.

"By following the Vedic rituals or undergoing atonement, sinful people do not become as purified as by chanting once the holy name, for only by such praising can one awaken devotional service within the heart.

"The ritualistic ceremonies of atonement recommended in religious scriptures are insufficient to cleanse the heart entirely because after atonement one's mind again runs toward sinful activities. Only by praising the holy name of God can one eradicate the dirt from their heart completely.

"O servants of Yamarāja, we demand that you do not try to take him to your master for punishment.

"One who chants the holy name of the Lord is immediately freed from the reactions of unlimited sins, even if he chants indirectly [to indicate something else], jokingly, for musical entertainment, or even neglectfully. This is accepted by all the learned scholars of the scriptures.

"Although one may neutralize the reactions of sinful life through austerity, charity, vows, and other such methods, these religious activities cannot uproot the material desires in one's heart. However, if one serves God with unconditional love, they are immediately freed from all such contaminations.

"As a fire burns dry grass to ashes, so the holy name of the Lord, whether chanted knowingly or unknowingly, burns to ashes, without fail, all the reactions of one's sinful activities.

"If a person unaware of the effective potency of a certain medicine takes that medicine or is forced to take it, it will act even without their knowledge because its potency does not depend on the patient's understanding. Similarly, even though one does not know the value of chanting the holy name of the Lord, if one chants knowingly or unknowingly, the chanting will be very effective."

The order carriers of Lord Vishnu then released the brāhmaṇa Ajāmila from the bondage of the Yamadūtas and saved him from imminent punishment.

Having been released from the nooses of Yamarāja's servants, the brāhmaṇa Ajāmila, now free from fear, came to his senses and immediately offered respects to the Vishnudūtas by bowing his head at their feet.

After hearing the discussion between the Yamadūtas and the Vishnudūtas, Ajāmila could understand that the transcendental principles concerning the relationship between the living being and God superseded all mundane religious rituals. His consciousness now purified, he could remember his past sinful actions, which he much regretted.

Ajāmila felt embarrassed for having wasted most of his life pursuing sense gratification and how he shamelessly rejected his previous spiritual training to abandon his pious wife and beget children in the womb of a prostitute. He even abandoned his mother and father who were dependent upon him as their only son.

He could now understand that his destiny was set to be punished for his sinful life but wondered if this vision he just experienced was merely a dream. "I saw fearsome men with ropes in their hands coming to arrest me and drag me away. Where have they gone?"

"And where have those four liberated and charming persons gone who released me from arrest and saved me from being dragged down to the hellish regions?"

He surmised that because of his previous spiritual activities, those four exalted personalities had come to rescue him and he felt exceedingly gratified.

"Were it not for my past devotional service, how could I have gotten an opportunity to chant the holy name of God when I was just about to die?" he concluded.

"I have been such a sinful man, but since I have now gotten this opportunity, I must completely control my mind, life, and senses and always engage in devotional service from here on out so that I may not fall again into the ignorance of mundane life.

"Because of identifying oneself with the body, one is subjected to desires for sense gratification, and thus one engages in many different types of pious and impious action. Being a most fallen soul, I was bewildered and became like a dancing dog led around by a woman's hand. I shall henceforth give up all lusty desires and free myself from this illusion and become a merciful, well-wishing friend to all living beings and absorb myself in spiritual practice."

With just a moment's association with the Vishnudūtas, Ajāmila was inspired to detach himself from the material conception of life with determination. Thus freed from all material attraction, he immediately started for the holy city of Hardwar where he resided at a Vishnu temple and practiced devotional yoga by controlling his senses and fully applying his mind and body in the service of the Lord.

When his intelligence and mind were purified, Ajāmila once again saw before him those four celestial beings, and thus he offered them his respects by bowing down before them.

At that moment, Ajāmila gave up his material body at Hardwar on the bank of the Ganges and regained his original spiritual form.

Accompanied by the order carriers of Lord Vishnu, Ajāmila went directly to the spiritual abode of Lord Vishnu, the husband of the goddess of fortune.

As you can see, the story of Ajāmila is miraculous, and according to the author, the great sage Vyasadeva, this very confidential historical narration has the potency to vanquish all sinful reactions and one who hears or describes it with faith and devotion, will never see the Yamadūtas at the time of death.

Sleep Paralysis

I first learned about sleep paralysis when I was experimenting with astral projection. I was 16 at the time, and the idea of moving into another dimension fascinated me. I had experienced what most people term, "Sleep paralysis" and it was frightening. However, I wanted to face my fears and understand what exactly was taking place when my body felt paralyzed while I remained conscious in bed.

It turns out, although the house I was living in was haunted by disembodied spirits, my sleep paralysis was not these ghosts trying to hold me down, but rather just an imperfect exit during an unconscious astral projection.

You see, when we sleep at night, our astral form (made up of our mind, intelligence and false ego) carries our soul outside of our physical body to recharge itself in the astral plane. Typically, these sleep paralysis experiences happen during the time when the astral body is beginning to leave the physical form, and right at that moment, we become conscious of the transition. Normally, we would be in an unconscious state and this transition would take place without us (the soul) being aware. But those times when we are aware and begin to panic, the astral body gets stuck halfway in and halfway out of the physical body, leading to a kind of paralysis, wherein, we do not have full control of the physical form and due to our conditioning, that is the only form we are aware of.

We've all had a similar experience when we've laid down a particular way as to cut off the blood flow within our leg or arm and experienced a "dead limb." As the sun rays illuminate the universe, similarly, our soul illuminates our body by the spread of consciousness in the form of *prana* (life force) that flows throughout our body in the form of blood. When this blood flow gets cut off, consciousness disappears from that part of the body and we experience a dead limb.

In the *Bhagavad-Gita*[12], Krishna explains:

---

[12] *Bhagavad-Gita As It Is,* verse 13:34 (BBT)

> *O son of Bharata, as the sun alone illuminates all this universe, so does the living entity, one within the body, illuminate the entire body by consciousness.*

My Astral Projection Experiences

I remember the first time I successfully did an astral projection while laying down in my room one afternoon. One of the techniques is to focus on your pulse in different parts of your body as the body slips into a sleep state. The focus kept me fully aware as my astral form started to carry me outside of my physical form. I first heard a ringing sound as my consciousness started to tune into the astral frequency, and then as I entered the astral dimension I looked down to see my physical body still laying on the bed. I felt as if I had left the planet and was entering a whole new world. I was excited and a bit fearful at the same time. My mind was racing, "Could I come back?" "Where am I going?" and then I heard two voices break through that completely freaked me out, "Look at him, he thinks he's good." These strange voices were mocking me and in a state of panic, within seconds, I came back into my physical form. There were people there watching me as I experimented. I was not alone in my room.

Many years later, I was a 31-year old monk traveling on a train through Siberia when I became aware of my astral body leaving my physical form as I entered into a sleep state. Rather than panic this time, I entertained the experience and decided to take full advantage of it. I consciously willed myself completely out of my physical form and urged myself up into the heavens. Suddenly, I was racing up at what felt like the speed of light. Stars and galactic forms raced passed me as I surged through the heavens, sometimes passing through iridescent tubes and sometimes the open night sky. It was incredible and then suddenly, I stopped moving and appeared in someone's home. But this was not earth. I had become an observer in someone else's home on a distant planet. I listened to their conversation and apparently they were aware of my presence and did not seem to mind. They talked about me dismissively as if my visit was nothing new to them. I learned that the planet I was on was called Gomeda. Suddenly, I felt ill and made my way to their kitchen and began to throw up. At that point, I was instantly transported back to my physical form on that train traveling through Siberia. The thrill of traveling so fast through space without a rocket has fascinated me ever since.

Another time, I experienced and out-of-body moment while under the influence of the psychotropic drug psilocybin. I was only 19 at the time, but now 35 years later I can still vividly recall that experience as I walked through the Blackheath forest in NSW, Australia as "high as a kite". My body was walking along but I, the soul, was catching a ride on my body's shoulders. I could clearly feel that I was the "driver of the car," the "man behind the curtain pulling the strings," the "witness" if you will and that my body was just a vehicle for this given moment in time. I was not this body. It was as clear as day to me and this experience drove me to learn more. I later took to the teachings of the Vedas to understand what was really going on and why I currently had to experience life in a physical form. During this same experience we all became aware of a whole new realm of subtle beings, "Nature spirits" who were inhabiting the forests. They and the trees tried to talk to us. The chemical psilocybin had retuned our consciousness to a whole different frequency and what was unseen and unheard before now appeared to us as clear as day. Our consciousness was now moving across a much wider band of frequencies. There was much more to our world than what our physical eyes and ears had revealed to us before.

It is important to understand here that just like there are many physical forms and levels of consciousness in the physical realm, similarly, there are many levels of consciousness (awareness) in the subtle realms. What most people experience of the subtle realms are the lower astral levels where you'll find souls in temporary astral forms (ghost bodies) because of having died in an intoxicated state, sudden death through an accident or gross attachment to a physical place or peoples. These forms are temporary, like all forms in the material world, but there are much more awakened subtle forms like nature spirits, devas and angels, for example. Each of them are evolving and performing service of some kind.

So if you've ever experienced sleep paralysis, do not panic. It is one of the ways God is teaching us that we are not these physical forms. We are spirit and this physical state of being is a temporary phase we all must pass through as we evolve in consciousness. We've all had many physical forms and so the sooner we can wake up to the fact that we are of a higher nature – spirit – and that our real home is in the higher spiritual realm, the faster we can progress and not have to take birth again.

Learning The Art Of Detachment

Let's face it, we all have to die. The quip, "Nothing is absolute in this world except death and taxes" is legitimate. Similarly, every living thing in this world, will at some point in time be forced to change bodies. This is also an absolute fact. So how does a soul prepare for such change? Just like anything, we must practice for that monumental moment.

You cannot expect to be ready for such a dramatic shift in circumstances unless you have consciously prepared yourself throughout your life. The basis of this preparation is detachment or renunciation. However, we can only cultivate renunciation by first understanding what it truly means.

As I have already pointed out, we enter this world empty-handed and leave it the same way, so what in fact do we really own? Truth be told, we are simply borrowing things for a set period of time, according to the law of karma. Once that period has expired, we are forced to renounce it – no exceptions. So, if in fact, we are just borrowing things, how can we possibly renounce anything? You cannot renounce something you don't own. In verse 5:29 of the *Bhagavad-Gita* Krishna offers a clue in His peace formula and it all centers around understanding the truth of ownership.

The sages, knowing Me as the ultimate purpose of all sacrifices and austerities, the Supreme Lord of all planets and demigods and the benefactor and well-wisher of all living entities, attain peace from the pangs of material miseries.

In other words, Krishna (God) emphatically declares that He is the true owner of everything in this material creation. By understanding this, a devotee of Krishna is able to practice true renunciation and this, my friend, is the key to detachment and preparation for dying.

Introspective souls will prepare for death by gradually reducing their attachments, renouncing unnecessary things, gifting other things in charity, reducing sensual gratification, fasting, and meditating on God's holy name. In this way, they fine tune their consciousness and disentangle themselves from material bondage.

Great sages in India, would leave their ashrams to live simply in the forest, while yogis would fast themselves to death. Apparently, fasting is the most dignified way to prepare for impending death, because with fasting, one shuts down all the typical bodily functions and with less things to be concerned about, like defecating, they are able to fully focus their consciousness on God.

Finally, according to the law of karma, at the time the soul enters a particular body, they are awarded a set number of breaths before the body expires and the soul is forced to evacuate. Your final breath, therefore, has been predetermined, however, the circumstances surrounding how you expire this last breath is not predetermined.

Death can come at any moment and so it behoves an introspective person to be aware of this fact at all times and to live their day as if it is their last one, for one day, it will be.

AFFIRMATION 2

I now know that death is simply the changing of form.
I am immutable. The state of my consciousness at
the time of death will determine my next form.

Maxim 3

We are Absolute Consciousness

"Consciousness cannot be accounted for in physical terms. For consciousness is absolutely fundamental. It cannot be accounted for in terms of anything else."
– Erwin Schrödinger

Einstein Was Partly Correct

Einstein's theory of relativity has been the foundation for modern physics for decades. He set the framework for understanding the deceptive nature of time and space and attempted to explain the so-called "law of gravity" in the same way.

However, it turns out that although Einstein was right about some things, many of his conclusions have since been proven wrong and his famous declaration of a "Theory of Everything (*ToE*) completely eluded him. Despite these failings, he is still glorified throughout the world as one of the greatest minds in the modern era.

Many conspiracy theorists believe Einstein was a hoax and that his theories were propped up to support an atheistic mechanistic worldview. Whereas, Tesla, the real genius of the 20th century, who famously disagreed with many of Einstein's conclusion, and who was an avid theist, was marginalized and practically erased from history. If not for the Internet, most people today would know nothing of Tesla's achievements, since he is non-existent in standard text books in schools around the world.

The Theory Of Everything

The **theory of everything (ToE)**, also known as the final theory, master theory, or ultimate theory is a hypothetical all-encompassing, single, coherent theoretical framework of physics that attempts to fully explain and tie together all physical aspects of the universe.

Identifying this elusive so-called "Theory of Everything" is an enormous challenge to modern physicists but absolutely critical for legitimizing all their other frameworks. Over the past three hundred years, only two theoretical frameworks have emerged as contenders for ToE and they form the foundation of all modern physics – **general relativity (GR) and quantum field theory (QFT).** The GR theoretical framework focuses on gravity for understanding the universe by looking at big things like stars and galaxies, etc. Whereas, QFT focuses on non-gravitational forces for understanding the universe by observing the nature of small scale and low mass: sub-atomic particles, atoms, molecules, etc. In other words, one method looks at the macro world while the other looks at the micro world.

QFT proponents have successfully presented the so-called "Grand Unified Theory" between the three non-gravitational forces, namely: weak, strong, and electromagnetic.

Through years of research, physicists have at least *experimentally* confirmed virtually every prediction made by these two theories when applied in their appropriate domains. However, these same scientists have openly admitted that GR and QFT, as they are currently understood, are not mutually compatible and therefore, cannot both be correct. Since the usual fields of applicability of GR and QFT are so different, most situations require that only one of the two theories be used.

To resolve this incompatibility, a new theoretical framework is needed to unify and harmoniously integrate GR and QFT into a seamless single theory that, in principle, is capable of describing all phenomena. In pursuit of this agenda, another concept called quantum gravity is actively being researched.

In the 1980's a single explanatory framework, called "string theory", was hailed as a possible theory of the universe. String theory posits that an instant after the so-called "Big Bang", the four fundamental forces (standard gravity, weak gravity, strong gravity and electromagnetic) were once a single fundamental force. According to string theory, every particle in the universe, has a unique combinations of vibrating strings with a specific pattern of vibration and that it is through these vibrating patterns that a particle of unique mass and force charge is created which set off a chain of reactions that led us to the complex life forms we have today!

However, John Ellis, Professor of Theoretical Physics at the Kings College in London and who is mostly credited with popularising the notion of a ToE, said: "Quite frankly, it is a little bit of an embarrassment that nobody in the 40-years since it was formulated has come up with a sensible way of testing string theory as a potential Theory of Everything. And I think that is an absolutely essential feature of any scientific theory that it should be testable."

Scientist Or Speculators?

One thing that rings true here, is that these scientist, well-meaning or not, are just speculating. None of them know for certain what the true nature of this universe is. They hypothesise based on experiments they have made in their laboratory or observatory and then extrapolate that out to the furthest distances of the known universe, both micro and macro, which then forces them to make an assumption that certain events must have taken place to enable their theories to work, as in the case of assuming events surrounding the so-called "Big Bang," which these same physicists speculate happened about 13.8 billion years ago.

With String theory not even being "testable," mundane science has no solid contender for the Theory of Everything, with many scientists suggesting that finding a ToE is like trying to find the end of the rainbow. However, many particle physicists stubbornly assert that the search for "dark matter" and new particles at CERN in Geneva are the "keys" to revealing the missing pieces that will lead them to a ToE, and of course as long as they keep that hope alive, they can continue requesting billions of dollars from taxpayers to fund their speculations.

Perspective Is Everything

What if instead of believing the latest speculation out of the mouths of theoretical physicists, we turn to the honest writings of the great sages and saints of the Vedas to get some insight into the nature of this material world and a "Theory of Everything" from a transcendental perspective.

This material world is certainly relative, in the sense that food for one man may be poison to another. This same logic is true for all areas of material existence. For example, if I held the palm of my hand facing out and asked you to look at my hand, you will see my palm, whereas, I will see the back of my hand. Both of us are viewing the same hand but are getting an entirely different perspective. That is the nature of this world, everything is relative in terms of our sensual capacity to measure things. However, if we view things from the spiritual perspective a different set of rules comes into play – rather than just seeing the hand, we see the owner of that hand – the soul within – that animates the body of which the hand is attached to. In other words, we see the complete picture and isn't that essential for arriving at a "Theory of Everything?"

Whereas, physical life is characterized by birth, disease, old-age and death; spiritual life (or the nature of the soul) is characterized by eternality, blissfulness and wisdom. As souls, we are a form of energy that is unfailing, flawless, and never-ending.

From the perspective of soul, this physical world is imperfect and temporary. Its purpose being to provide a stage for the eternal soul to play out a particular persona under the influence of a perverted ego. It's this kind of radical, paradigm-shifting thinking, that is needed to truly find a unified theory to explain this mysterious experience we call life.

By nature, the body is ever changing, and the soul is eternal. This understanding is accepted by all classes of seers of the truth, both the personalist, who believe in a divine Creator and the impersonalist who espouse that the Absolute Truth has no form. In both cases, they acknowledge the eternality of the soul.

In fact, understanding that the soul is eternal and not destroyed even after the demise of the body is the beginning of self-realization. However, even with multiple academic accolades many scientists don't understand it, nor do they care to understand. Ironically, they are the one's sleeping through life, beholden to their prestigious positions in society.

In the *Bhagavad-Gītā*, Krishna declares to Arjuna:

> *As the embodied soul continually passes, in this body, from boyhood to youth to old age, the soul similarly passes into another body at death. The self-realized soul is not bewildered by such a change.*[13]

> *As a person puts on new garments, giving up old ones, similarly, the soul accepts new material bodies, giving up the old and useless ones.*[14]

If we accept the Vedic conclusion as stated in the *Bhagavad-Gītā* that these material bodies are perishable in due course of time and that the soul is eternal, then we must remember always that the body is like a suit or dress; therefore, why lament the change of clothing?

In a dream we may think of flying in the sky, or driving a fast car, but when we wake up we can see that we are neither in the sky nor sitting in a car. The Vedic seers encouraged self-realization

---

[13] *Bhagavad-Gita As It Is,* verse 2:13 (BBT)
[14] *Bhagavad-Gita As It Is,* verse 2.22 (BBT)

on the basis of the illusion of a material body. Therefore, in either case, whether you believe in the existence of the soul or not, there is no cause for lamentation for loss of the body. In other words, we will either live on as souls, or we will become food for worms. In both cases, there is nothing we can do to change these facts.

The material body has no factual existence in relation to the eternal soul. It is something like a dream, and believe it or not, science is starting to embrace this concept.

Mind Over Matter

The interplay of our thoughts with the material world is of tremendous interest today, amassing increasing attention by academics worldwide. Despite an abundance of scientific data proving that the mind can influence matter, as well as the clear connections of how emotional states can lead to chronic illness, most people who work in mainstream medicine remain entirely ignorant of these facts.

The most well-known experiment that proves these connections is the placebo effect. This effect is remarkable because it genuinely does unlock the power of the mind. The biological changes observed in the body after conducting a placebo test are not triggered by the placebo, but rather by the mind, our perception, and our psychological response to the fake placebo treatments.

A study appearing in the scientific journal, *Brain, Behavior, and Immunity* documents that the mind does play a role in both cancer growth and recovery. Patient trials suggested that stress management interventions do reduce inflammation and in animal studies, stress hormones made a range of cancers spread faster.[15]

Researchers all over the world have discovered that placebo treatments do stimulate real biological and physiological

---

[15] (https://www.sciencedirect.com/science/article/pii/S088915911400 0658)

responses, including changes in blood pressure, heart rate and even chemical actions in the brain. Harnessing the power of the mind, the placebo effect has been effective in treating arthritis, Parkinson's disease, fatigue, anxiety, and more.

Dogma Does Not Equal Truth

The current scientific dogma is heavily grounded on assumptions that are associated with classical physics, despite the fact that over a century ago physicists discovered empirical phenomena that could not be explained by classical physics.

During the 1920s and early 1930s a revolutionary new branch of physics called quantum mechanics (QM) evolved to address these new discoveries.

In 2014, leading scientists, from a variety of scientific fields (biology, neuroscience, psychology, medicine, and psychiatry), participated in an international summit in Tucson, Arizona on post-materialist science, spirituality and society. The result of that gathering was the *Manifesto For a Post-Materialist Science*[16] which stated in part:

> "QM explicitly introduced the mind into its basic conceptual structure since it was found that particles being observed and the observer—the physicist and the method used for observation—are linked. According to one interpretation of QM, this phenomenon implies that the consciousness of the observer is vital to the existence of the physical events being observed, and that mental events can affect the physical world. The results of recent experiments support this interpretation. These results suggest that the physical world is no longer the primary or sole component of reality, and that it cannot be fully understood without making reference to the mind."

---

[16] http://opensciences.org/about/manifesto-for-a-post-materialist-science

Furthermore, the *Manifesto* pointed out the resistance of some scientists and philosophers to welcome empirical data that challenged their theories.

> "Some materialistically inclined scientists and philosophers refuse to acknowledge these phenomena because they are not consistent with their exclusive conception of the world. Rejection of post-materialist investigation of nature or refusal to publish strong science findings supporting a post-materialist framework are antithetical to the true spirit of scientific inquiry, which is that empirical data must always be adequately dealt with. Data which do not fit favored theories and beliefs cannot be dismissed a priori. Such dismissal is the realm of ideology, not science."

The *Manifesto* boldly suggested that a more inclusive post-materialistic (read: spiritual) attitude was critical to the preservation of humanity and our planet:

> "The post-materialist paradigm has far-reaching implications. It fundamentally alters the vision we have of ourselves, giving us back our dignity and power, as humans and as scientists. This paradigm fosters positive values such as compassion, respect, and peace. By emphasizing a deep connection between ourselves and nature at large, the post-materialist paradigm also promotes environmental awareness and the preservation of our biosphere. In addition, it is not new, but only forgotten for four hundred years, that a lived transmaterial understanding may be the cornerstone of health and wellness, as it has been held and preserved in ancient mind-body-spirit practices, religious traditions, and contemplative approaches."

What Is Truly Absolute?

While we may comically suggest that "death and taxes" are absolute, nothing is absolute in this physical realm – everything is in a constant state of flux. The only thing that is truly absolute is that we (as souls) do not actually die and that the soul is immutable. The soul's eternality is confirmed by Krishna in the *Bhagavad-Gita* verse 2.20.

> *For the soul there is never birth nor death. Nor, having once been, does he ever cease to be. He is unborn, eternal, ever-existing, undying and primeval. He is not slain when the body is slain.*

Grasping with the concept of eternality is never easy. We are conditioned from birth to think in terms of beginning and end. We see birth and death everywhere we look. We are ruled by time and schedules. Eternality, although believable, is a very hard concept to grasp, and yet our higher-self screams for it to be true. We feel it is true. None of us can actually imagine what death is. You might suggest it is just darkness or an "eternal sleep state," but even in describing it that way we have to use the word eternality which challenges the concept of time itself and if we go into a sleep state, who is sleeping? Furthermore, to sleep means that at some point we were awake; to be in darkness means there is light somewhere else; to cease to be means that at some point we were. Death, in all of its finality, feels alien to us as souls. And in reality, it is. Death is really just a changing of perspective. At some point in time, a body is animated by the presence of a host soul, and then at another point in time, that soul moves away from that body, not unlike a person leaving a house who is then given a new body (home) to inhabit based on that soul's desires and karma. The soul remains the same, albeit wiser, but the situation or perspective has completely changed.

Don't Worry So Much

Worrying has never solved anyone's problems. On the contrary, it has only led to increased mental anguish, degrading health and a downward spiral of loss and destruction.

Once you understand your nature as an eternal soul and that this physical experience is just one of millions you have gone through already, then worrying about anything becomes a trivial and tragic waste of time.

A study conducted in 1990 presented indirect evidence suggesting that worry was principally thought-like in content. In an academic paper, *The Nature, Functions and Origins of Worry*[17], T.D. Borkovec of Penn State University suggests that perhaps the most important and fundamental characteristic of worry is that it involves a type of internal verbal-linguistic activity, i.e., thinking.

When asked what proportion of their worrisome experience is predominantly thought, imagery, or a mixture of these two cognitive events, 900 community women indicated 51%, 3%, and 46%, respectively; when asked in a format forcing a choice between thoughts and images[18].

When subjects were asked to characterize the feeling states that they typically experienced when worrying, the majority of their worries (46.9%) related to the future, implying anticipated threat, as opposed to the past (20.9%). Fear of making mistakes, of being criticized, and of meeting people rank among the highest, specific, anxiety-provoking events.

We can therefore conclude that worry is a predominantly an internal dialogue to avoid future aversive events. Its chronic and severe forms emerge in people who perceive the world to be a dangerous place and who are afraid that they will not be able to cope with what the future holds for them.

The paper concludes that applied relaxation combined with cognitive therapy and/or visualization techniques and

---

[17] https://www.academia.edu/952382/The_nature_of_normal_and _pathological_worry
[18] (Borkovec & Lyonfields, 1993)

desensitization techniques (such as float tanks and meditation) yielded significant and long-lasting benefits to people prone to worry.

This tendency to worry needs to be channelled into constructive pro-active actions and words that will lessen the apparent calamities on the horizon. If you have reason to worry about something, rather than just worrying, get up and do something now. Focus all your mental and physical energy in avoiding that imaginary monster inside your head. Granted, you may be in real danger, and so the need to be pro-active is even greater. So stop worrying and start doing.

Embrace Change

Change is as natural as the wind. In the *Bhagavad-Gita* verse 2:14, Krishna explains to his friend, Arjuna that the temporary appearances of happiness and distress in our lives are like the changing seasons. They come and go. Nothing remains the same forever and so a true yogi is not disturbed by these changes but is tolerant.

> *O son of Kunti, the nonpermanent appearance of happiness and distress, and their disappearance in due course, are like the appearance and disappearance of winter and summer seasons. They arise from sense perception, O scion of Bharata, and one must learn to tolerate them without being disturbed.*

We see change everywhere. This material world is constantly changing. Death becomes birth and birth leads to death. Our bodies age over time, while we, "the witness" remain the same. Our mothers still envision us as their baby and yet we now have aging adult bodies. Their love for us manifests in their innate ability to connect to our essence – our spirit identity – seeing through the layers of skin and bone. So while everything material is destined to change, one thing that does not change is our spiritual identity, for it is transcendental to this material energy.

The Temporary World of Names

India's *Bhagavat Purana*, also known as the *Srimad Bhagavatam* verse 2.2.3 has an interesting take on the nature of this material world.

> *For this reason, the enlightened person should endeavor only for the minimum necessities of life while in the world of names. He should be intelligently fixed and never endeavor for unwanted things, being competent to perceive practically that all such endeavours are merely hard labor for nothing.*

The whole material creation is nothing but a puree of names that delude us into believing that things made up of the same material elements (earth, water, fire, air and ether) are somehow different. The buildings, furniture, cars, houses, factories, electronics, etc., are all just names given to the same material elements. Externally, these things manifest in different ways but if we look at them energetically, they are hardly distinguishable.

So while it is important to make such distinctions for matters of social convention and conformity, it is imperative that we not lose sight of the true nature of this material world. Everything is energy that is changing shape but the names we use to describe things gives them a sense of permanence that is unjustifiable in the grand scheme of things.

It is critical that you learn to see the "inside story" of life and not just the "book cover" of false ego. Look deep within and tune into the higher frequency of who you really are. See the absoluteness of soul – your true self and embrace your brilliance as a spark of God's splendour. This material world may indeed be relative but you, as a soul, are not. You, I and every living thing is absolutely an eternal spirit soul expressing itself through forms.

AFFIRMATION 3

I am absolute. While my material form is transient my essence as the "witness" remains the same. I do not worry about the future but embrace the optimism of now.

Maxim 4

Evolution of Consciousness Begins When We Master Our Tongue

"Deliver my soul, O LORD, from lying lips, and from a deceitful tongue." - Psalms 120:2 KJ21

Learning To Control The Senses

When we hear gurus tell us to control our senses, our natural tendency is to cringe and squirm in protest. After all, enjoying is part of life. It motivates us to work hard and push beyond our so-called "limits." I mean, we have to be happy! So what is wrong with sensual gratification? Well, there is certainly nothing wrong with enjoying, for bliss is the nature of the soul. In fact, enjoyment is the primary motivator of life. What is needed is to learn how to enjoy in such a way as to not exploit or take the life of another living being.

So "controlling the senses" does not mean we should stop enjoying, it simply means we have to regulate and master our senses so that they do not degrade our consciousness.

From the age of 19 until 33 I was a celibate monk. I slept on the floor, used my hands or a folded up cloth as my pillow, took only cool showers and ate three vegetarian meals cooked by temple priest at scheduled times. I limited my interaction with women so much that I would barely look them in the eye and often look at their feet instead.

The craziest part of my story is that for a few years during my life as a monk I did fundraising for the temple and one of the things we sold to maintain the temple was perfume! Yes, the temple president at that time was running an incense and scented oil business called *Spiritual Sky* and decided to dabble in commercial perfume. He created a brand called *John Aurelie* and imported bottles from France, marked MADE IN FRANCE to dupe the Australian public into thinking the perfumes were also made in France. Myself and about 10 other monks would venture out into the business districts of Australian cities and go door-to-door selling these perfumes. In the beginning we actually donned wigs to cover our bald heads and dressed in stylish business attire. Later, we kept very short hair and wore caps.

Well, you can imagine the situation was not at all conducive to a celibate life with beautiful women fawning over the perfumes and saying all kinds of sexual innuendos to try to get a discount. I remember one lady looking me directly in the crutch and asking, "can you come back at 5pm and show me what you've got?" I didn't.

Another time, I foolishly found myself inside a brothel surrounded by 5 scantily clad young women all wanting to try the perfume. I could feel my energy being drowned by their sexual intensity and I packed up and left, saying that I had an important call to make. I had to take a cold shower, do a headstand for 10 minutes and chant a few hundred mantras to get over that experience.

All of us monks struggled at various times but somehow the majority of us made it through unscathed, although, all but a handful of us eventually got married. In the tradition I followed, it was perfectly normal for a monk to get married at some point. You were never expected to remain celibate for life. Typically, a boy of 5 years was given over to the guru to be trained in spiritual life. He lived at the guru's school (Gurukul), practiced celibacy and studied the scriptures while living a very regulated life. At the age of 25, a boy was then encouraged to wed, unless he was considered strong enough to remain celibate for the rest of his life. In my case, I started this tradition at the age of 19, and decided to get married at the age of 33.

Looking back now, I am proud of my achievement for it was certainly not easy to live such a life during the prime years of a man's life and venturing out from the sanctity of the temple was always like playing with fire. But I was able to completely abstain from sex and masturbation from the age of 19-33. How? I learned the art of mastering the tongue.

In the Vedic literature it is mentioned that in order to understand Krishna (God), one has to engage all the senses in acts of devotion and the most important sense is the tongue. If one can control (read: master and regulate) the tongue, they have the best chance of controlling all the other senses.

It is also described in the *Bhagavad-Gita* that one can only give up the lower taste by experiencing the higher taste. In other words, there is no possibility of giving up sex unless one is experiencing a superior pleasure.

"Of all the senses, the tongue is the most voracious" wrote Bhaktivinoda Thakur a prolific Vaishnava scholar and poet from West Bengal. "But you, my dear Krishna have given us *prasadam*, just to control the tongue." Thakur was a married man with many children and was not your stereotypical holy man, however, he lived a noble and regulated life of devotion to God, while performing his civic duties. He understood the importance of mastering the urges of the tongue and would only eat food that was first offered to God and chanted the holy name of Krishna for many hours a day.

Prasadam, of course is sanctified plant-based food that has been offered in devotion to Krishna and according to the tradition, those that partake of such *prasadam* are purified of all their sins.

Tasting

The tongue has two functions: tasting and vibrating. As a monk, I learned very fast just how critical it was for my vow of celibacy to never eat too much or too little, and to avoid foods that would agitate my mind and senses. I was taught that there is a direct line from the tongue to the stomach to the genitals and so if I could control my eating habits, that would help tremendously in controlling the urges of the stomach and genitals.

I found this to be true and so I kept a strict habit of never overeating and avoiding stimulating foods like chili and desserts.

However, we're all naturally motivated and hard-wired to eat and enjoy foods that bring us sensual gratification so regulating our eating is never easy. I mean, who wants to go to a party and not eat cake!? Well, for the most part, that is exactly what I did. Even at our temple festivals where there was an overabundance of desserts, I refrained and only took small portions. The point here is to never eat more than you can comfortably digest. Know your limits, and if you happen to be practicing celibacy as I was, dial it in bigtime. You really have to control the urges of the tongue.

Karma-Free Eating

When I joined the temple, one of the first things I was told by the other monks was, "You can eat your way back to the spiritual world." I am like, "What?" "Are you serious?" "Yes, because all the food we prepare in the temple has been offered in devotion to Krishna and therefore it has been transformed and is now spiritual, so the more you eat the more purification you get."

Thinking back to those times, I laugh at how gullible I was. Yes, food can be transformed energetically, and I document this in my other book, *FOOD YOGA – Nourishing Body, Mind & Soul*, however, our material body has a limit and until such time that we can fully transcend the entrapment of having a material form we must honour it accordingly, and that means, understanding it's limitations.

Initially, it is perfectly fine to indulge oneself during the early days of celibacy as we try to distract our attention away from the female form and focus on transcendental subjects. Gorging on blessed food is a great distraction and because it is energetically different from your regular run-of-the-mill food it does purify your consciousness. However, eventually, the day comes when your body lets you know that enough is enough and you have to regulate and control your eating.

The reality is that we can only eat so much. We could be presented with a smorgasbord of delicious foods from all over the world and yet our stomachs are only so big. Alas, that is the nature of the material world. Our desires may be enormous, but our capacity to enjoy is limited.

We see this frustration of limitation in the lives of Hollywood celebrities that have enormous wealth, and spending habits to match, and yet they are controlled by alcohol and pharmaceutical drugs in a fruitless pursuit of trying to enjoy beyond their natural capacity.

The bottom line here is that although it is perfectly natural to want to enjoy, since it is the innate characteristic of the soul, the real goal of life is self-realization. In the human form we have a tremendous capacity for raising our awareness of our higher self so that at the time of death we can ascend out of this material frequency and not have to take birth again. So the rule is: Enjoy responsibly while keeping it real.

Vibration

The other characteristic of the tongue is to vibrate. Making sounds with our tongues is what we have all been doing since birth. It is natural and it is our most effective way to communicate. However, it also happens to be the most effective way to transform our consciousness.

You see, the words we speak are literally writing the screenplay of our lives. Words are vibrations, vibration is energy, and energy has the power to change things.

Think about this: every World War; every divorce; every failing relationship; and every opinion or perception has been shaped and initiated by someone's words.

Words are seeds. Words can paint a picture of perfection or a masterpiece of doom. Words can heal and words can wound. Words can uplift and words can destroy.

The essence of the *Law of Attraction* is based in the words we use to paint our future. We do that by projecting our consciousness into a future of happiness, prosperity and abundance while living in the now. "We fake it until we make it." We act and speak as if our ideal story is here now and we do that using choice words.

So to control the tongue it requires that we not only regulate and be aware of our food choices but also that we be conscientious of the words we speak. Both functions have to mastered.

It is said in the *Bhagavad-Gita verse 17:15*:

> *Austerity of speech consists in speaking truthfully and beneficially and in avoiding speech that offends. One should also recite the Vedas regularly.*

Commentator on the *Bhagavad-Gita* Srila Prabhupada writes:

> One should not speak in such a way as to agitate the minds of others. Of course, when a teacher speaks, he can speak the truth for the instruction of his students, but such a teacher should not speak to others who are not his students if he will agitate their minds. This is penance as far as talking is concerned. Besides that, one should not talk nonsense.

Speech is the most important quality of any person. It is said that a fool may be dressed like an intelligent man but as soon as he speaks, he reveals himself at once.

William Shakespeare famously wrote: *"A fool thinks himself to be wise, but a wise man knows himself to be a fool."* While Confucius is attributed with saying: *"True wisdom is knowing what you don't know"*

The idea being presented here is that our self-awareness is always lacking and that there is always more to learn. It is impossible to know everything and knowing our limitations is the hallmark of a wise man. The successful man or woman remains a student throughout life, and as a result, they continue to progress.

Affirmations

Affirmation are not a new concept although they have been popularized by books like *The Secret*. In fact, affirmations have been a pillar of every spiritual tradition and yet, for the most part, today we don't see people using them on a regular basis.

Most likely this is due to the ubiquitous nature of marketing and news that controls how most of us think and feel. We are being told what to wear, eat and think every minute of the day.

An affirmation by nature is a command to the Universe or God to manifest something desirable in our life. It is a direct challenge to material nature to drastically change your reality. An affirmation can be a stick in the spoke of the wheel of destiny or a masterpiece of happiness brought forth through shear will. In all cases, however, we have to be detached and allow the affirmation to manifest in divine timing.

That is something I learned first-hand when I was a monk, even before I understood the Law of Attraction or the power of focused intention and manifestation.

While trying to raise funds for the temple, I would set myself a target at the start of the day and send that command out to the Universe as a matter of fact. I would say, "I already have $1000 in my pocket" and I would repeat this statement hundreds of times throughout the day. As a result, it would dramatically shift my attitude to that of abundance and when I approached people to sell my products, I was completely detached and confident. I walked confidently; I talked confidently and I would look people directly in their eyes and shake their hands firmly. Sure enough, by the end of the day, I had collected exactly if not more than $1000.

I didn't know it at the time but that was my first attempt at affirmations.

To create your own personal affirmation, you just have to follow these rules:

1. Write and speak in the present tense as if it has already happened
2. Speak exactly what you desire
3. Allow that thing to manifest in divine timing
4. Be detached
5. Feed your affirmation with gratitude

The following notes are inspired by the writings of Kelsey Aida, author of *How to Make Your Own Badass Positive Affirmations*.

I AM...

Two of the most powerful words in the English language. If the affirmation is for personal change than start it with "I AM".

Craft yourself as you wish to be.

I AM THANKFUL FOR...

Practicing gratitude is the fastest way to raise your vibration and attract more things to be thankful for.

I EMBRACE, ENJOY, LOVE, LIKE (INSERT GOOD FEELING ADJECTIVE HERE)

Start your affirmation with this when you're feeling good about something. Embrace it, encourage it, and express how much you love it. Admiring the good things in your life will elevate your mood, attitude, and attract more of the same good things in.

I FORGIVE…

When you forgive you are choosing to rise above the entrapment and toxicity of anger. Whether you're forgiving a friend, family member, your boss, or yourself, forgiveness will set you free and create space for inner success.

I CHOOSE…

Choose what you want for yourself and show God that you are taking responsibility and charge for your life. The Divine will conspire to make it happen for you.

I AM WILLING TO…

Being willing is one of the most admirable qualities in the eyes of God. As soon as you are willing to see thing differently, willing to let go, or willing to dream big, the Divine will support you in that willingness. Soon enough that willingness will blossom into intention and then a firm decision and then conviction.

I CAN…

Maybe you're not exactly where you'd like to be right now, but you sure can be if you choose! You can be, do, or have anything you can conjure up in your imagination. Anything! God in your heart would never seed you an idea that could not be fulfilled. Of course, you absolutely must believe this thing to be your destiny with 100% conviction.

I LET GO OF/ I RELEASE…

Sometimes, when you're feeling beaten down the best thing to do is simply to surrender. Let go of it. You may have reached a point where you're too exhausted to change your mind or accept anything. So release it to relieve your burden.

Kirtan

When I was a monk I learned about the ancient practice of kirtan, or the congregational chanting of the holy name of God. In the tradition I followed, we primarily chanted the *Hare Krishna mantra, Hare Krishna Hare Krishna, Krishna Krishna Hare Hare, Hare Rama Hare Rama, Rama Rama Hare Hare*

Essentially, this mantra is made of three words, Hare, Krishna and Rama. Hare means "energy" and is also representative of the Divine Feminine (Radha). Krishna means "the all attractive one" or the Divine Masculine and Rama means "the source of happiness" and is also likened to service since unconditional service is the currency of true happiness.

So putting this altogether we get the following mantra in English:

"Oh Divine Feminine, Oh Divine Masculine, please engage me in your loving service."

According to the tradition, the Hare Krishna mantra is not an ordinary sound; it is *para-prakti* (pure sound) and not of this material world.

We would also chant many other mantras and all of them were essentially inspiring us or encouraging our devotion to Radha and Krishna.

Chanting mantras and specifically performing kirtan can be a powerful experience. Very quickly you are swept up in the positive energy of the group and your consciousness is purified. As a monk, I would do kirtan for at least 2 hours a day and personal chanting of mantras (japa) for at least another 2 hours every day.

In the *Bhagavad-Gita* verse 9:14 Krishna declares that the great souls (mahatmas) are:

> *Always chanting My glories, endeavoring with great determination, bowing down before Me, these great souls perpetually worship Me with devotion.*

Praying Ceaselessly

Even in the Christian tradition, ceaseless prayer is encouraged. The first thing to note here is how the bible, as do other spiritual traditions, recognize that the Lord's name is holy. In other words, it is not of this world, it is transcendental.

Matthew 6:9-13 (the Lord's prayer[19]) – "In this manner, therefore, pray: Our Father in heaven, *Hallowed be Your name.* Your kingdom come. Your will be done on earth as it is in heaven. Give us this day our daily bread. And forgive us our debts, as we forgive our debtors. And do not lead us into temptation, but deliver us from the evil one. For Yours is the kingdom and the power and the glory forever. Amen."

Then there are these lesser known statements:

1 Thessalonians 5:16-18 – "Pray without ceasing. In everything give thanks, for this is the will of God in Christ Jesus concerning you."[20]

Matthew 26:40-41 – "And He [Jesus] came unto the disciples and found them asleep, and said unto Peter, "What, could ye not watch with Me one hour? Watch and pray, that ye enter not into temptation. The spirit indeed is willing, but the flesh is weak.""[21]

Samuel 12:23 (Samuel speaking to Israel) – "As for me, far be it from me that I should sin against the Lord by failing to pray for you. And I will teach you the way that is good and right."[22]

The apostle Paul is probably one of the busiest people in his time – evident in the many accomplishments that he had – yet he was the one who encouraged believers to pray nonstop. So this praying ceaselessly in the Christian tradition is no different from the kirtan tradition of chanting the holy name continuously.

---

[19] New International version (NIV)
[20] 21st Century King James Version (KJ21)
[21] 21st Century King James Version (KJ21)
[22] New International version (NIV).

AFFIRMATION 4

I am a master of my tongue. I eat with compassion
and speak words that are truthful, inspiring
and beneficial to myself and others.

Maxim 5

You Are A Creator

---

*"Raise your words, not your voice. It is rain
that grows flowers, not thunder." -Rumi*

Changing The Programming

We live in a world ruled by cliché and dopamine-triggering social
media "truths" in the form of memes. We repeat rather than
create. We forward or share news feeds without thinking, and we
cling to cognitive dissonance as if our life depended on it.

For the most part, most of us are on auto-pilot, digesting
whatever is thrown at us, not questioning the narrative and like
a soul-less echo-chamber we repeat back what we heard without
conscience.

I am sure you know people like this and hopefully, you dear
reader, are not one of them.

The first step in awakening to your full potential is to take
control of your life and that includes your mind. We have been
programmed from birth to think a certain way. Some of this
programming is even genetically coded, which makes it that
much more difficult to change, but believe me, you can even
change your genetic coding.

Certainly, using affirmations and controlling your tongue to
only speak words that are uplifting, truthful and healing is a step

in the right direction, but to really initiate change at a cellular level we have to go deeper into the subconscious.

We also have to take heed of every kind of food we consume and every person we associate with and every sound we expose our mind and body to.

Don't Speak What You Don't Want

The opposite is also true. If you don't want poverty; if you don't want disease or some other challenging situation, do not "feed" it with confirming sound vibration.

If you happen to find yourself short of money or not feeling well, don't speak of the challenge as if it is an absolute fact of your reality. Rather, speak of it as something that is temporary, which in fact, it is. You see, nothing remains the same in this world. Things and situations are always in a constant state of flux. Everything ages, erodes, or changes form. Similarly, our material body may at some point in time succumb to disease but soon enough it passes once the body has had a chance to address the issue through the natural healing process.

Or you may find yourself short of cash or even homeless but we all know that if you put enough effort in, there will be a new opportunity to earn money and a bed to sleep on.

So rather than claiming, "I am always broke," say, "At this time, I may be short on funds but that will not last for long. Soon enough I will have the funds I need." And then make a concerted effort to rectify your financial situation. In other words, don't just talk about it (although our words are certainly the "seeds" of creation) but act as well.

The point is to practice speaking what you want and avoid speaking or "feeding" what you don't want.

The Ancient Manifesting Ritual

I learned this technique from Sarah Prout, a long-time manifesting expert. The ritual dates back many hundreds of years and is a form of magical invocation, using the power of the written word.

The ritual requires that you be in a state of flow, in other words, your energy has to be calm and open to transformation. You need to find a quiet place where you will not be disturbed for around 30-60 minutes. It is critical that you first calm your mind through deep breathing and find a comfortable place to sit and write.

You should have a special notepad and pen to use for this ritual. The first step is sit quietly and meditate on what is the most important need in your life. Is it financial abundance? Is it a loving relationship? Is it your health? Focus on that urgent need and conjure up a present-tense manifestation that you can easily write down in one sentence. It is also important that you write the manifestation in the present-tense as if it has already happened. Typically, that will mean starting your manifestation with I AM, I AM GRATEFUL, I AM HAPPY, I AM RELIEVED, etc.

For example, my first attempt at this ritual was to write: I am grateful that my relationship with Juliana is now perfect.

I believed that this sentence (intention) captured my sincere desire succinctly.

The next step is to write this statement down 55 times and to repeat this exercise for the next 5 days in a row. You want to imprint this command in your subconscious and let it go. Do not meditate on it any further. Let it go and allow it to manifest in divine timing. You should only do one manifestation at a time, so if you have another urgent need, then repeat this process over another 5 -day period.

I would recommend doing this very early in the morning. I would do this and then after writing the manifestation 55 times I would then chant the Hare Krishna mantra 108 times to bless the intention.

I then created a geometric signature of this manifestation which is the exact sentence mapped to a magic square of the sun.

Manifestion #1

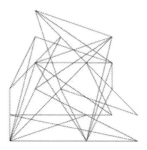

I AM NOW GRATEFUL THAT MY RELATIONSHIP WITH
JULIANA IS NOW PERFECT

What Is A Geometric Signature?

A geometric signature, also known as a *soul yantra* is a unique contribution to the ancient sigil (talisman) traditions. Like the traditional yantras and Talismans, a geometric signature is also based on the sciences of numerology, magic squares, geometry, and astrology. However, in this case, the encoded data is not a call to some Archangel, as in the case of sigils used in the magic traditions but is representative of a particular affirmation.

In the same way that numerology can encode a person's character and aptitudes in numbers, the geometric signature does so through geometry. A geometric signature literally captures an affirmation in a harmonic geometric pattern that can then be used as aid to meditation. To learn more about geometric signatures, visit www.soulyantra.com

Poor Health Choices Begin In The Mind

It is suggested in India's Ayurvedic texts that all disease begins in the mind.

When a person is depressed, the whole body is negatively impacted. Depressed people get ill easier and the road to recovery is more challenging. People who are happier and more positive are typically better able to fend off diseases and enjoy better health during a chronic illness.

It appears that the author of the Ayurveda, Vyasadeva was onto something – negative thoughts are like "seeds" that if cultivated can mature into full blown diseases. Obviously, there are many factors that contribute to disease but our emotional health plays a significant role.

Everyone feels sad once in a while but depressed people often lose interest in normal activities such as eating and exercise, and their sleeping patterns are disrupted leading to poor decision making.

The National Institute on Aging rocked the medical world with the results of a remarkable study that tracked 4,825 people ages 71 and older. Researchers found that those who were chronically depressed for at least six years had an 88 percent greater risk of developing cancer within the next four years. The researchers wondered if depression fuelled cancer by damaging T-cells and other parts of the body that fight the disease, although they also considered that both cancer and chemotherapy may have biochemical effects that contribute to depression as well.

Even before doctors had any idea that mood could affect a person's chances of getting cancer, it was already clear that depression and loneliness added to the devastation of the disease once it was present.

The state of our mind does impact our physical health and we all have our personal experiences to attest to this fact.

Your body will respond to the way you think, feel, and act. When you are stressed, anxious, or upset, your body reacts in a way that might tell you that something is wrong. For example, you might develop high blood pressure or a stomach ulcer after a particularly stressful event, such as the loss of a loved one.

A weak or disturbed mind can weaken your body's immune system, making you more susceptible to colds and other infections during emotionally-challenging times. Also, when you are feeling anxious, stressed, or upset, you may not take good care of your physical body. For example, you may not feel like exercising, eating nutritious foods, or taking the medicine that your doctor prescribed. You may also abuse alcohol, tobacco, or other lifestyle drugs.

Health-related quality of life (HRQOL) has been well documented to impact both self-reported chronic diseases (diabetes, breast cancer, arthritis, and hypertension) and their risk factors (body mass index, physical inactivity, and smoking status)[23].

Aside from the negative impact poor emotional health can have on our physical body, there is also the danger of developing bad habits that can lead to poor health.

Sound Is The Basis Of Creation

Everything manifest begins with the utterance of a word. Every world war; every divorce; every bridge or skyscraper that was ever built; every invention; every child that was born, all started with sound. The creation of that thing first started in a sound form.

"Though often too low or too high for human ears to detect, insects and animals signal each other with vibrations. Even trees and plants fizz with the sound of tiny air bubbles bursting in their plumbing," writes Besky Oskins of *Live Science*.[24]

> Sound is so fundamental to life that some scientists now think there's a kernel of truth to folklore that

---

[23] Centers for Disease Control and Prevention. Measuring healthy days: Population assessment of health-related quality of life. Centers for Disease Control and Prevention, Atlanta, Georgia 2000.

[24] *Sound Garden: Can Plants Actually Talk and Hear?* https://www.livescience.com/27802-plants-trees-talk-with-sound.html By Becky Oskin, Contributing Writer | March 11, 2013

holds humans can commune with plants. And plants
may use sound to communicate with one another.

"If even bacteria can signal one another with vibrations, why
not plants," said Monica Gagliano, a plant physiologist at the
University of Western Australia in Crawley.

"Sound is overwhelming, it's everywhere. Surely life
would have used it to its advantage in all forms," she told
OurAmazingPlanet.

According to the Ancient Vedic texts, the original seed of
creation was the sound of "OM", also written as AUM or OUM,
which denotes the divine trinity of creation. In the Bible, it is
stated, "in the beginning was the word, and the word was God,"
clearly illustrating that creation was initiated through sound.

OM is both a sound and a symbol rich in meaning and depth
and actually consists of three syllables: A, U, M.

The first syllable is A, pronounced as a prolonged "awe." The
sound starts at the back of your throat.

The second syllable is U, pronounced as a prolonged "oo," with
the sound gradually rolling forward along your upper palate.

The third syllable is M, pronounced as a prolonged "mmmm"
with your front teeth gently touching.

The oṁkāra praṇava or OM is considered to be the sound
incarnation of the Supreme Personality of Godhead. "As such,
oṁkāra is eternal, unlimited, transcendental, supreme and
indestructible," writes A.C. Bhaktivedanta Swami Prabhupada.

"Oṁkāra is the beginning, middle, end, and the beginningless.
When one understands oṁkāra as such, he becomes immortal
because oṁkāra is a representation of the divine Lord situated
in everyone's heart."

"By understanding oṁkāra one can become free from the
duality of the material world and attain absolute knowledge.

Therefore, oṁkāra is the most auspicious representation of the Supreme Lord," states the Māṇḍūkya Upaniṣad[25].

According to Prabhupada, Oṁkāra is as good as any other manifestation of the Supreme Lord.

> The Lord has innumerable incarnations, and oṁkāra is one of them. As Krishna states in *Bhagavad-Gītā*: "Amongst vibrations, I am the syllable om." (Bg. 9.17) This means that oṁkāra is nondifferent from Krishna.

> Oṁkāra is therefore the ultimate representation of all the Vedas. Indeed, the Vedic mantras or hymns have transcendental value because they are prefixed by the syllable om. The Vaisnavas interpret oṁkāra as follows: by the letter O, Krishna, the Supreme Personality of Godhead, is indicated; by the letter U, Krishna's eternal consort Śrīmatī Rādhārāṇī is indicated; and by the letter M, the eternal servitor of the Supreme Lord, the living entity, is indicated.

Everything in the universe is pulsating and vibrating – nothing is standing still. The sound OM, when chanted, vibrates at the frequency of 432 Hz, which is the same vibrational frequency found throughout everything in nature and interestingly it is also 4 x the sacred number 108.

It is stated in the Vedic literatures that the creator of this universe we live in, Lord Brahma has 4 heads which corresponds to the 4 fundamental dimensions of space, up, down, left and right. The number 108 is considered to be the divine key to unlock the mysteries of sacred geometry and it also has significant spiritual significance in that is the recommended number of chants one should do of the sacred mantras.

OM is the basic sound of the universe; so by chanting it we

---

[25] The Māṇḍūkya Upaniṣad (Sanskrit: माण्डूक्य उपनिषद्, is the shortest of all the Upanishads, and is assigned to Atharvaveda. It is listed as number 6 in the Muktikā canon of 108 Upanishads.

are symbolically and physically tuning in to that sound and acknowledging our connection to all other living beings, nature and the universe.

From *Srimad-Bhagavatam* we learn that when Brahma, the first created being, first awoke after having been created, he found himself seated on a great lotus, surrounded by cosmic darkness and wondered what it all meant.

He looked in all directions in bewilderment and wonder but finally, amidst that darkness, he heard a transcendent sound from the Personality of Godhead, the gayatri mantra[26]. Acting on the instructions contained in that mantra, he steadied his mind in meditation and at last saw before him a vision of the spiritual realm and the Personality of Godhead, Krishna.

By the grace of Krishna, he could now understand everything about his own self, his purpose in life, the lotus, the darkness—everything. He was then inspired to create the universe we currently reside in. Brahma is the original creator of the known universe and his actions were prompted by sound.

It seems that Brahma's curiosity laid the fertile soil for which the "seed" of the divine creative sound could be planted.

The Secret Behind The Secret

The Law of Attraction promoted in books like *The Secret,* is nothing new. The concept of manifesting what you desire through focused intention and words is a technique that has been practiced since the beginning of creation. You see, even before there is sound, there must be focused intention, or at least in Bramha's example, a sense of genuine curiosity – in other words, a sincere desire for answers or change.

When we focus our intention, we essentially laser-focus our heart's desire into one singular outcome. All other things

---

[26] The *Gāyatrī*, also known as the *Sāvitrī* mantra, is a highly revered mantra from the Rig Veda (Mandala 3.62.10), dedicated to Savitr, the sun deity. https://en.wikipedia.org/wiki/Gayatri_Mantra

dissolve to the background and a singular picture comes into focus. Imagine you are using a camera with a high-powered lens, you select an object in the distance and start dialling the lens to focus in on that one thing. As you do, everything else fades from the picture. That is the kind of focused intention we are talking about.

In a practical sense, when we focus our intention, we have to clear our mind of all other thoughts. This may require practice but it is well worth the effort. It is the kind of discipline that all successful leaders have perfected. Talk to any successful athlete or business person and they will tell you the same thing, "I knew I would be successful." Why do they say that? Because their intention was so focused that that is all they could see in their mind's eye. That goal of success became their guiding light. It was all they could see and so it became their reality. Soon enough, that mental reality gradually manifested in the real world.

None of this is magic. It is just how things work in this world and to fully understand why it works this way, you have to get clear on why we are here in the first place.

When I was a monk, one of the first things I learned was the nature of the soul. You can imagine that taking up the life of a monk at the tender age of 19 is not easy. Celibacy is difficult at any age but 19 when the hormones are raging is another thing entirely!

The only way I could possibly do this was through understanding the nature of my true self and to continually remind my mind of that truth. I was an eternal soul, the "witness" or "driver" of the body. The body was not me but simply the vehicle I was currently using to express myself at this time.

Of course, this intellectual adjustment had its limits. There was no denying the urges of the body so we would also practice yoga asanas like headstands, carefully monitor our diet, regulate our eating habits and keep a respectable distance from all women. It was not uncommon for us monks, when addressing a women to look them in the eyes for the briefest moment to acknowledge their presence and then for the remainder of the discussion to look only at their feet.

Those monks that were successful were the ones that were able to develop a focused intention and maintain their awareness as souls. It was not easy but it was doable and I managed to maintain my vow of celibacy for 14 years.

The Intention Experiment

There is plenty of scientific research to support the efficacy of focused intention. Lynn McTaggert's ground-breaking book, *The Intention Experiment* documents research conducted at Princeton, MIT, Stanford, and other universities and laboratories to reveal that intent is capable of profoundly affecting all aspects of our lives. In the book, William A. Tiller, a professor emeritus at Stanford University, argues: "For the last 400 years, an unstated assumption of science is that human intention cannot affect what we call physical reality. Our experimental research of the past decade shows that, for today's world and under the right conditions, this assumption is no longer correct."

McTaggart describes much of the evidence and the theory behind psi and intention experiments in her books *The Field: the Quest for the Secret Force of the Universe* and *The Intention Experiments: Using Your Thoughts to Change Your Life and the World*, as do Greg Becker and Harry Massey in their documentary film *The Living Matrix: The New Science of Healing*.

Most of these researchers believe there is some kind of nonlocal, universal energy field that connects human beings in a vast web of relationships with each other and with everything in the creation. In other words, we are interconnected beings. When a thought twitches one strand in the universal web, strands in other parts of the web vibrate in response – a kind of harmonic resonance, if you will, similar to how strings on a harp vibrate in harmony. A single thought may have an infinitesimally small effect, but the collective brain of humanity can radiate inconceivable numbers of intentions and thoughts every second, forming a global mind and having a cumulative effect that can alter the state of consciousness of a city, country, planet, and perhaps even of the universe at large.

Quantum physics offers that there is a universal ground field, also known as the zero-point field or the lowest possible energy state of atoms from which particles and anti-particles blip in and out of existence.

Some scientists and philosophers speculate that the zero-point field is also an information field with a kind of "memory" that holds data about everything that has ever happened in the universe. The zero-point field sounds very similar to the Akashic records talked about by the ancients.

British biologist Rupert Sheldrake believes there is a "morphogenetic field"[27] that provides a template for matter, with each species of life having its own template to direct its growth and shape its characteristics.

Although our intention may be a measurable force, it may not be the actual mechanism by which we influence physical matter. Harry Massey, executive producer of the documentary *The Living Matrix: The New Science of Healing*, explains the dynamics this way:

> "Intention seems to be a linking process, not an extracting process. For example, if you intend to connect with a person who is at a distance to send them a healing frequency, the intention is the connection point. Something more is going on that is allowing information transfer to take place. Intention seems to get you to the point where information can be accessed and transferred, but intention itself does not fully explain the mechanism for the transfer."

Whatever the relationship between intention and information transfer, most neotic and many leading physicists agree that

---

[27] Morphogenesis is the biological process that causes an organism to develop its shape. It is one of three fundamental aspects of developmental biology along with the control of cell growth and cellular differentiation, unified in evolutionary developmental biology

human consciousness may be the most fundamental aspect of the universe. According to the Vedic literatures of India, consciousness is a symptom of the soul, much like the sun rays are to the sun globe and since the universal creation is but the dream of Vishnu, the zero-point energy field is believed to be dream state of Vishnu shaping the universe, moment by moment.

The evidence clearly shows that consciousness can extend outside of the physical body, so it is highly unlikely that it is just an emanating property of our brains. One classic example of this is the phenomena known as the "phantom limb" which is the sensation that an amputated or missing limb is still attached. Most amputees experience the "phantom limb" syndrome in their amputated limb and the majority of the sensations are painful. I can verify this since at the age of 16 I lost the top of my right index finger and for many years after I felt that the top of the finger was still physically present.

Our thoughts and intentions can influence not only the state of our minds and quality of our lives but also our physical health. It's astonishing to think that what we think about others and the energy we project toward them, may actually affect them on a physical level. It's also curious that our beliefs play a role in how effectively we can use our focused intention in specific, directed ways, giving credence to the notion "as we think, so goes the world."

The quantum interconnected theory of consciousness is shared in one form or another by most of the major thinkers in the fields of psi research, consciousness research, and even frontier medicine, biology, and physics, including psychoneuroimmunologist Candace Pert, systems theorist Ervin Laszlo, IONS founder and former astronaut Edgar Mitchell, physicians Larry Dossey and Deepak Chopra, cell biologists James Oschman and Bruce Lipton, and physiologist and director of research at HeartMath Rollin McCraty.

As McTaggart writes in *The Field*,

> "We are not isolated beings living our desperate lives on a lonely planet in an indifferent universe. . . .We

were always part of a larger whole. We were and always had been at the center of things. Things did not fall apart. The center did hold and it was we who were doing the holding."

Her sentiment is echoed by Marilyn Mandala Schlitz, director of IONS, as follows:

". . .As you begin to think about this kind of quantum model . . . as a metaphor it begins to impact how we think about reality. It's clear that rather than thinking about ourselves as separate from each other and separate from the world outside of ourselves that we begin to think of ourselves as entangled relationship-centered entities, that we're not alone and that anything we do has consequences not only for ourselves but for the world outside of ourselves-because that world isn't really outside of ourselves."

If you are like most people, you may find this knowledge of interconnectedness inspiring. Just imagine the kind of world we could create if we all begin taking responsibility for our thoughts and intentions and focused and directed them for the greater good?

Like all significant undertakings, it all begins with a first step, so start cultivating a positive and focused intention for the good of yourself and the world today and join with the global mind to shift the very condition of our world.

Like the great Lord Brahma, we are also creators, only on a much smaller scale.

AFFIRMATION 5

I am an important player in the universal web. My intentions and words have power. I use them responsibly to create a positive and beneficial effect in this world.

Maxim 6

Connect with Mother Nature

---

*"Earth and sky, woods and fields, lakes
and rivers, the mountain and the sea,
are excellent schoolmasters, and teach
some of us more than we can ever
learn from books." - John Lubbock*

Modern Society Has Lost Touch

Today, millions of people live in high-rise apartment blocks around the world. In Moscow alone, there are 11,783 high-rise towers, in Hong Kong there are 7,833, and in Seoul there are over 7,000, many of which are residential. In Singapore, between 1960 and 1976, the percentage of people living in high-rise buildings climbed from 9% to 51%. Despite the general perception that living in skyscrapers is seen as a status symbol, many feel an absence of community, despite living alongside hundreds or thousands of other people.

These "boxes" in the sky, deny a natural connection to Earth and with the modern invention of the rubber souled shoe, we have a human population that very rarely even has skin contact with Earth.

In 2007, Professor Robert Gifford of the University of Victoria, published an article, *"The Consequences of Living in High-Rise Buildings,"* in the journal *Architectural Science Review*. Dr. Gifford's manuscript surveyed nearly 100 studies that investigated whether high-rise living improved or diminished well-being and mental health.

Each study focused on answering a question about whether living in tall buildings increased or diminished housing satisfaction, psychological stressors, suicide, behavioural problems, crime and fear of crime, positive social relations, or healthy child rearing.

The results were discouraging. Of the 99 studies reviewed, only 17 measured a positive outcome for the research question; 55 measured negative effects, and 27 were mixed or neutral. Across these different categories, a large number of studies found that people living in high-rise apartments suffered from greater mental health problems, higher fear of crime, fewer positive social interactions, and more difficulty with raising their children.

The report stated:

> More serious mental health problems have tenuously been related to building height. In an English study, mothers who lived in flats reported more depressive symptoms than those who lived in houses (Richman, 1974). Rates of mental illness rose with floor level in an English study (Goodman, 1974). Psychological symptoms were more often present in high rises (Hannay, 1979).

And on child rearing, he concludes:

> The problems range from fundamental child development issues to everyday activities such as play. For example, a Japanese investigation (Oda, Taniguchi, Wen & Higurashi, 1989) concluded that the development of infants raised above the fifth floor in high-rise buildings is delayed, compared to those raised below the fifth floor. The development of numerous skills, such as dressing, helping and

appropriate urination was slower. Children who live on higher floors also go outside to play less often (Nitta, 1980, in Oda et al., 1989).

Adding to the sense of disconnection high-rise residents experience, we have a modern world dominated by electronic communication where face-to-face meetings are losing their relevance, and with the introduction of various AI technologies this social handicap is not slowing down soon.

The Power Of Earthing Or Grounding

There are some practical things we can do to counter this modern disconnection.

Since the dawn of time, humans have had an intimate connection to the natural world, and this included walking barefoot. When the soles of your feet touch the ground, something miraculous takes place.

Long before we had *Air Nikes* or *Adidas* running shoes, our ancestors preferred to walk barefoot over dirt, rubble, and grasses. Their feet would have been strong, nimble and sensitive so that they could quickly sense and react to any surface they encountered. More recent native cultures preferred to walk barefoot as well.

Our ancestor's preference for "barefootedness" begs the question, "why?" when even in more recent times, simple footwear was an option.

Thankfully, there has been some solid scientific research into walking barefoot and the findings are fascinating.

What researches discovered is that the benefits we get when our feet make direct contact with the earth is more than just a feeling. The curative touch of mother earth is laden with astonishing health benefits, such as improving sleep, reducing inflammation, promoting healthy blood flow, and even clearing the body of electromagnetic radiation.

The ancient practice of walking barefoot, sometimes referred to as "grounding", is only just beginning to be studied by modern science, but one of the most promising discoveries is the effect that a direct contact of our skin to earth can have on our heart health.

According to a 2013 study published in the *Journal of Alternative and Complimentary Medicine*, walking barefoot "reduces blood viscosity, which is a major factor in cardiovascular disease".

Blood viscosity is a measure of the thickness and stickiness of your blood. The lower the viscosity, the easier your blood circulates throughout your body.

To measure whether grounding the body to the earth's innate electrical charge would have a positive effect on blood condition, a group of subjects had their red blood cells (RBCs) examined under a microscope to determine the number of clumped groups of RBCs in each sample. High instances of clumping in human blood increases the blood viscosity and can result in cardiovascular disease.

They discovered that walking barefoot substantially lowered blood cell clumping in every one of the subjects and promoted healthier circulation.

A later study in the same journal found that spending some time directly touching the earth may help regulate both the endocrine and nervous systems as well.

Modern-day humans have to battle through a proverbial stormy ocean of electromagnetic waves radiated by Wi-Fi, mobile phone signals, and a host of other electronic conveniences, etc. This "dirty electricity" or "electromagnetic pollution" is nothing to take lightly and yet for most people, they don't even think twice about it, simply because it is invisible.

By divine arrangement, the earth's surface is rich with electrons that can neutralize this electromagnetic pollution and bring the natural currents within our bodies back to a healthy balance.

Nikola Tesla once stated: "Our entire biological system, the brain, and the Earth itself, work on the same frequencies."

We often laugh at the simplicity of our ancient ancestors, but it is foolish to think that the current generation has it all figured out. Sometimes, the answer to good health is sitting at our feet.

However, there are other natural methods to achieve the same benefits as grounding and one in particular may surprise you.

According to the ancient Vedas of India, the cow is the personification of Earth. She is literally Earth with legs. Similarly, the bull is considered to be like a "father" figure.

While lying on the ground or walking barefoot for a few minutes at night can do wonders for relieving stress and curing insomnia, believe it or not, but hugging a cow or a bullock has the same effect and it is way more fun! It will not only cleanse your electrical body of unwanted dirty electricity; it will also distress you.

Cow hugging is a recognized healing modality that has been practiced for thousands of years in India.

I encourage you to take a visit to your local animal sanctuary and hug a cow or a baby calf. Try this out and see for yourself how relaxing it is.

If you do not live near protected cows, then I suggest you try a grounding mat. The system is to place a copper pipe in the ground, connect a wire to it and run it into your home and attach that wire to a grounding mat. You then place your feet on this mat when sitting down or using the computer. Alternatively, you can connect the wire to the grounding (earth socket of your electrical outlet).

The Importance Of Water

Of all the elements, water is the most important.

It is commonly recommended to drink eight 8-ounce glasses of water per day, although there is little science behind this specific rule. Staying hydrated is important and the Mayo Clinic recommends that people should drink around 1 litre of water per 30kg of weight.

The National Academies of Sciences, Engineering, and Medicine determined that an adequate daily fluid intake is:

About 15.5 cups (3.7 liters) of fluids for men and about 11.5 cups (2.7 liters) of fluids a day for women. Please note that the total water intake recommended is the **sum** of plain drinking water, and water from formulas, beverages, and foods consumed.

Other than athletes, most people are unaware that water helps to maximize physical performance, particularly during intense exercise or high heat.

Dehydration can have a noticeable effect if you lose as little as 2% of your body's water content. Athletes, therefore, must rehydrate regularly during heavy workouts or competition.

Dehydration can lead to reduced motivation, increased fatigue and make exercise feel much more difficult, both physically and mentally. This is not surprising when you consider that muscle is about 80% water.

Your brain is also impaired by dehydration. Studies have shown that even mild dehydration can sometimes dramatically impair many aspects of brain function.

In a study of young women, fluid loss of 1.36% (of body weight) after exercise impaired both mood and concentration, and increased the frequency of headaches[28].

In another study on young men, it was discovered that "mild dehydration without hyperthermia in men induced adverse changes in vigilance and working memory, and increased tension, anxiety and fatigue."[29]

A 1-3% fluid loss equals about 1.5 to 4.5 lbs (0.5 to 2 kg) of body weight loss for an average 150 lbs (68 kg) person. This kind of fluid loss can easily occur through normal daily activities, let alone during exercise or high heat.

Drinking an adequate amount of water can help to prevent and treat headaches. Considering the fact that our brain is about 90% water this claim has merit. Several studies have shown that water can relieve headaches in those who are dehydrated.[30]

Drinking enough water may help relieve constipation,

---

[28] https://www.ncbi.nlm.nih.gov/pubmed/22190027
[29] https://www.ncbi.nlm.nih.gov/pubmed/21736786
[30] https://www.ncbi.nlm.nih.gov/pubmed/14979888

characterized by infrequent bowel movements and difficulty passing stool. Although usually the biggest factor is a lack of fibre in the diet of which the highest sources of fibre are fruits and vegetables that also contain a lot of water.

It has also been documented that kidney stones, or clumps of mineral crystal that form in the urinary system have been reduced with sufficient quantity of water consumption. One study indicates that increased water intake reduces the risk of recurrence of urinary stones and prolongs the average interval for recurrences.[31]

Higher fluid intake increases the volume of urine passing through the kidneys, which dilutes the concentration of minerals, so they are less likely to crystallize and form clumps.

Drinking sufficient amounts of water can help with weight loss, due to the fact that water can increase satiety and boost your metabolic rate.

Drinking 2 litres of water every day can increase your total energy expenditure by up to 96 calories per day, and more importantly, drinking water half an hour before meals and not during meals is the most effective.

In one study, dieters who drank half a litre of water before meals lost 44% more weight, over a period of 12 weeks.[32]

The Spiritual Significance Of Water

However, there is much more significance to water than the physical benefits it brings. In his commentary of the *Srimad Bhagavatam*, Srila Prabhupada writes:

> "The construction of the whole material world is prominently made by three elements, namely earth, water and fire. But the living force is produced by sky, air and water. So water is the common element

[31] https://www.cochranelibrary.com/cdsr/doi/10.1002/14651858. CD004292.pub3/full

[32] https://www.ncbi.nlm.nih.gov/pubmed/19661958

in both the gross and subtle forms of the material creation. Water is the most prominent element and is therefore the principle element of all the five." [33]

In my book, *FOOD YOGA – Nourishing Body, Mind, and Soul* I explain that as a transporter of energy, water has the ability to heal when it is pristine, or to make us sick if it carries bacteria. Nothing is as essential to life as clean water, and yet our supply of clean water is dwindling before our eyes. As water becomes scarcer on our planet, the question must be asked: "Are we failing to hear its message? Is water trying to communicate to us?" said the late Dr. Masaru Emoto, author of *The Hidden Messages in Water* and *The True Power of Water*. These questions motivated Dr. Emoto's groundbreaking discovery of how water communicates to us.

Dr. Emoto surmised that if our bodies are made up of mostly water, and if water can be so easily influenced, it follows that the vibrations we expose our bodies to can literally change our lives. The music we listen to, the movies we watch, the environment we live in, and the people we associate with – all affect our physical, mental, and even spiritual health to some degree.

All of these environmental influences are essentially energy vibrations, impacting our physical, mental and spiritual bodies. You have probably experienced that after watching a particularly violent movie, you came away feeling uneasy or agitated. Conversely, after spending time in the park, among the trees and animals, you feel refreshed and enlivened. There is a stark contrast between the vibrations that each environment emits. Like air, radio, and TV waves, water is also a conduit of influence. Indeed, the ancient healing modality of homeopathy is based on the belief that was has memory.

Emoto believed that water is the messenger of God, or a "conduit of Spirit," and that one can improve the quality of their life by "sending healing energy to water." To pray to water, he

---

[33] - *Srimad Bhagavatam* 2.10.31 commentary. (BBT)

postulates, is the same as praying to God, because "water is an expression of God."

Emoto's research led him to India, where he took water crystal photos from the holy River Ganges. "The quality of the water was not so good physically," he explained, "yet we could obtain a beautiful shaped water crystal." He speculates that this was probably a result of the multitude of prayers offered from people around the river. Interestingly, in support of Werner Heisenberg's "Uncertainty Principle," he also offered that, had the photographer been Hindu and revered the River Ganges, "then even more beautiful water crystals could have been obtained." This, of course, is due to the influence of the observer's vibration.

Emoto discovered that water changes its expression when exposed to particular words and intentions, and that the words "love" and "gratitude" had the most profound impact on the water he tested. He noted that the impact was even greater when the words "apology" and "forgiveness" were spoken with heartfelt sincerity.

When asked if he thought water was in some way conscious, Emoto explained, "...water seems to be receptive to harmonized vibrations and unreceptive to dissonant vibrations....It has the capacity to receive and reflect, inheriting a divine intelligence."

Of all the material elements, water is the one that speaks to our body, mind and soul. In its purest form it energizes our body through the process of hydrolysis; as calming tea it can still our mind; as a transporter of higher vibrations it can inspire our soul; and its feminine qualities can embrace and nurture our entire being.

Take the time to fully appreciate this wonderful element and reap the benefits of holistic well-being.

Sun gazing

Contrary to popular belief, the sun is not our enemy. In fact, sunlight is critical for our health, most significantly in helping our body produce Vitamin D. Although excess sunlight can contribute to skin cancers, a moderate amount of sunlight actually has preventive benefits when it comes to cancer.

Decreased sun exposure has been associated with a drop in serotonin levels, which can lead to major depression with seasonal changes. The light-induced effects of serotonin are triggered by sunlight that goes in through the eye. Sunlight cues special areas in the retina, which triggers the release of serotonin. So, you're more likely to experience this type of depression in the winter time, when the days are shorter.

Due to this connection, one of the main treatments for depression with seasonal changes is light therapy, also known as phototherapy. You can get a light therapy box to have at home. The light from the box mimics natural sunlight that stimulates the brain to make serotonin and reduces excess melatonin.

The system of sun gazing originated with Lord Mahavir of the Jain tradition, who practiced sun gazing over 2600 years ago. Sun gazing has also existed in ancient Egyptian, Greek, and Native American cultures.

Much is not understood about this ancient health practice. However, what is known is that gazing at the sun or exposing our body to high spectrum lighting activates the pineal gland, the gland responsible for the body's circadian rhythm. The pituitary was once considered a "master gland" until it was later discovered that it was actually controlled by the pineal gland. The pineal gland secretes melatonin, which is a powerful antioxidant; controls blood sugar and sleep rhythms, as well as the function of the pituitary gland.

Mr. Hira Ratan Manek, of Bodhavad, India began practicing the ancient system of sun gazing after retiring in 1995 and has and continues to live only on sun energy and water since that time! Occasionally, for hospitality and social purposes, he drinks tea, coffee and buttermilk. However, since 1995 he has performed three strict fasting sessions, all of which were strictly observed by independent medical and documentary teams from around the world, during which time he sustained himself exclusively on sun energy and water.

The first two of these fasting sessions in India lasted for 211 days, followed by a 411-day fast directed by an International team of 21 medical doctors and scientists.

After the reports of these fasts reached the US, Mr. Manek was invited to Thomas Jefferson University and the University of Pennsylvania in Philadelphia, where he underwent a 130-day observation period. This Science/Medical Team wanted to observe and examine his retina, pineal gland and brain. The observation team was led by Dr. Andrew B. Newberg, a leading authority on the brain who was featured in the movie *What the Bleep Do We Know*, and by Dr. George C. Brenard, the leading authority on the pineal gland. Initial results indicated that the grey cells in Mr. Manek's brain were regenerating. Seven hundred photographs were taken where the neurons were reported to be active and not dying. Furthermore, the pineal gland was expanding rather than shrinking, which is what typically happens in one's mid-50s, when its maximum average size is about 6 x 6 mm. Mr. Manek's pineal gland, however, was measured at 8 x 11 mm.

One explanation is that there seems to be a correlation between hemoglobin (in blood) and chlorophyll (in plants). Mason Howe Dwinell[34], a student of Manek, suggests "the effects of the sun on chlorophyll may be related to the effects of the sun on hemoglobin." Hemoglobin has the same chemical formula and function as chlorophyll, except that hemoglobin has iron (Fe) in its center, while chlorophyll has magnesium (Mg). This link between hemoglobin and chlorophyll and Manek's recommended 44 minutes of exposure to the sun to enable all the blood in the body to pass through the retinas[35] is still under research. It is not too farfetched, however, to think that the human body, much like a plant, could photosynthesize sunrays into energy that our body can use. Another interesting discovery relating to

---

[34] *The Earth Was Flat*, insight into the ancient practice of sun gazing, by Mason Howe Dwinell. 2005.

[35] The retina is the only place in the body where the sunlight touches the human blood vessels directly or almost directly.

sun gazing was made in 1979 when Fritz Hollwich showed [36]that light (electromagnetic pulse) entering the eyes helps regulate the autonomic and hormonal processes.

Fritz Hollwich, M.D. discoveries were expanded upon by Dr. Jacob Liberman [37]whom Hollwich praised as a "milestone forward regarding the therapeutic effect of light via the eyes."

Dr. Liberman explains:

> The Bible tells us that life began with the dawning of light, and virtually every spiritual tradition identifies light with the Creator, speaking of the "Divine Light" and the "Light of God," and describing the process of spiritual evolution as "enlightenment." Arriving at a realization is often referred to as "seeing the light," and health and wellbeing are usually accompanied by a physical radiance. This radiance is, in fact, a quantifiable phenomenon, known to scientists as biophoton emission or ultra-weak bioluminescence.

According to Liberman, Hollwich and later, in the practical example of Manek, the relationship between light and health begins in our eyes. When natural light enters the eyes, it travels through the brain directly to the body's "biological clock" located within the brain's brain, or hypothalamus.

Manek teaches that one should gaze at the sun only during the first hour of sunrise and during the remaining minutes of sunset for small increments of time, gradually increasing the sessions until a maximum exposure of 44 minutes is achieved. At which time, he claims, "one does not have to eat ever again!"

It is important to understand that Mr. Manek achieved his results in a very controlled environment under strict Jain principles. According to Manek, sun gazing is to be practiced standing bare footed on bare earth. You can stand on sand,

---

[36] *The Influence of Ocular Light Perception on Metabolism in Man and in Animal – Fritz Hollwich, 1979*

[37] *Light: Medicine of the Future* – Dr. Jacob Liberman, 1990.

gravel, stones, mud, or bare soil. Whatever is available. However, standing on tar, concrete, or grass, the results may be a bit slower.

Breathing

The science of breathing stands on quite ancient foundations. Centuries of wisdom instructs us to pay closer attention to our breathing, the most basic of things we do each day. And yet, maybe because breathing is so basic, it's also easy to ignore. A brief review of the latest science on breathing and the brain, and overall health serves as a reminder that breathing deserves much closer attention – there's more going on with each breath than we realize.

Controlling your breathing calms your brain and regulates your blood pressure. As I explained earlier, according to the ancient yoga teachings of India, at the time of our birth, we are allotted a certain amount of breaths for this life, so it follows then, that slowing down our breathing will increase our lifespan.

> In yoga we learn to control prana, the vital force, through pranayama. We use the breath in pranayama to learn to control prana, but don't confuse prana with breath. Prana is the energy that animates the lungs. It is not the breath. Using the breath is the easiest method for training prana. Once you are able to control prana through pranayama you are better able to control the movement of prana to other organs and areas of the body. – Amarajit Singh

In the 1930s, Nobel Prize winner Dr. Otto Warburg hypothesized,

> "Cancer has only one prime cause. The prime cause of cancer is the replacement of normal oxygen respiration of body cells by an anaerobic (oxygen-less) cell respiration."

He believed that cancer cells thrive in oxygen-poor environments and many research studies now support his assertion. Thanks to Warburg and others, we know that cancer cells metabolize differently than normal cells, which need oxygen for respiration. Instead, cancer cells metabolize through the process of fermentation. This inferior form of energy production is activated when the oxygen level of a cell drops below 40 percent. This leads to an acidic environment that encourages the growth of cancer cells.

It goes without saying that to get the full benefits of breathing practice, we should avoid smoking and also breathing in second-hand smoke. According to the CDC, "Second-hand smoke is the combination of smoke from the burning end of a cigarette and the smoke breathed out by smokers. Second-hand smoke contains more than 7,000 chemicals. Hundreds are toxic and about 70 can cause cancer. Since the 1964 Surgeon General's Report, 2.5 million adults who were non-smokers died because they breathed second-hand smoke."

During my time as a monk, we practiced mantra meditation and this required that we control and regulate our breath in order to chant effectively and steady the mind.

Learning to breathe the right way has been a staple of elite athletes for centuries. In fact, breathing is so important to master that two athletes might be matched in every other skill but the one that has the better cardio is typically the one who reigns victorious.

The Yoga Tradition Of Breath Control

Modern research is now confirming what yogis have known all along: Breathing exercises can deliver powerful benefits to our body and mind.

Despite the inherently automatic nature of breathing, there is much to learn and improve upon when it comes to the most basic of our physiological functions.

Most people breath from 14 to 20 breaths per minute, which is about three times faster than the 5 or 6 breaths per minute proven to help you feel your best, says Patricia Gerberg, MD, assistant clinical professor of psychiatry at New York Medical College and co-author of *The Healing Power of the Breath*.

Breath control, also known as pranayama, is the fourth of Patanjali's eight limbs of yoga. Scientific research is showing that mindful breathing is one of the most effective ways to lower everyday stress levels and improve a variety of health factors ranging from mood to metabolism.

"Pranayama is at once a physical-health practice, mental-health practice, and meditation. It is not just breath training; it's mind training that uses the breath as a vehicle," says Roger Cole, PhD, an Iyengar Yoga teacher and physiology researcher in Del Mar, California.

"There is a very direct relationship between breath rate, mood state, and autonomic nervous system state," says Sat Bir Singh Khalsa, PhD, assistant professor of medicine at Harvard Medical School who studies yoga and meditation.

Today's nonstop barrage of smartphone pings, emails, and news updates trips the body's autonomic nervous system that governs the body's fight-or-flight and rest-and-restore responses into action, impacting functions like heart rate, respiration, and digestion. Learning to control the breath can dramatically help us cope with all these abnormal stresses of modern living.

"We've long known that breath changes in response to emotion: When people get panicky and anxious, their breath becomes shallow and rapid," says Khalsa. "But we now know from a number of really good studies[38] that actively changing the breath rate can actually change autonomic function and mood state."

With each breath, millions of sensory receptors in the respiratory system send signals to the brainstem. Fast breathing pings the brain at a higher rate, triggering it to activate the sympathetic nervous system, turning up stress hormones, heart

---

[38] Effects of yogic breath regulation: A narrative review of scientific evidence
https://www.sciencedirect.com/science/article/pii/S0975947617303224

rate, blood pressure, muscle tension, sweat production, and anxiety. On the other hand, slowing your breathing induces the parasympathetic response, reducing all of the above and increasing relaxation, calm, and mental clarity.

Expelling carbon dioxide, not bringing in oxygen, is the main stimulus that drives us to breathe under most circumstances. Our body's urge to reject what it doesn't need is greater than its urge to acquire what it does. Simply because an excess of CO_2 makes the blood more acidic, which will impair the function of our body's cells. The natural function of the body to maintain the ideal pH of the blood triggers the stress response if the pH of the blood becomes too acidic, sending an urgent message to the diaphragm to initiate a breath to bring in more O_2 and rebalance the blood.

Eating The Way Nature Intended

For those of us that believe in a Divine Creator, there is no doubt that every part of the creation has been perfectly designed and this includes every human, animal, bird, bug, fruit, vegetable and grain on the planet. However, many humans have always thought themselves smarter than their Creator and they express that pompous attitude through the manipulation of the food we eat. Processed or "de-natured" foods have become a staple of the SAD (Standard American Diet) diet.

Granted, in many cases, there has been some value added with the ingenious innovations humans have brought to the food world, but at what cost? Some of the more radical changes, like genetic engineering may result in long-term damage to the human genome.

And there is the blatant de-naturing of food grains to the point that they are structurally altered and become nutritionally useless. Food processing uses strong acids, organic solvents or inorganic salts to change the structure of foods. Even when food is cooked it can alter the proteins, making it denatured, however, this is not to say that we should only consume raw foods, as the fact is, some foods require cooking and are even more nutritious when steamed, such as broccoli[39].

The real problem is that denaturation of foods causes a major change in nucleic acid and protein structures, resulting in disruption of cell activity and sometimes cell death. Many processed foods today have been denatured to the point that they lack any essential vitamins or minerals.

The Case Against GMO

Susan Brassard at the Livestrong website states: "The rise in autoimmune diseases, infertility, gastrointestinal problems and chronic diseases may be associated with the introduction of genetically modified foods (GM). In a position paper by the *American Academy of Environmental Medicine*, the authors ask all physicians to consider the role of GM foods in the nation's health crisis, and advise their patients to avoid all GM foods whenever possible. The Academy also recommends a moratorium on GM seeds and calls for immediate independent safety testing and the labelling of all food items containing genetically modified products."

In 2018, The United States Department of Agriculture proposed new guidelines for labelling foods that contain genetically modified ingredients. Food makers are now required by federal law to use labels, starting in 2020. Companies producing foods with GMO ingredients have fought hard for decades against such labelling laws out of fear that it would deter consumers from buying their products.

But what exactly will these labels say? Instead of the stigmatized terms "G.M.O." and "genetically engineered," the new GMO guidelines propose labels that say "bioengineered" or "BE." Food makers would be given a choice of three ways to disclose their methods, 1. spelling out the information, as in "contains a bioengineered food ingredient"; 2. using an icon (several logos

---

[39] See https://nutritionfacts.org/topics/broccoli/

evoking sun and smiles were proposed); or 3. affixing a QR code that directs consumers to a website with more information.

The new law simply states that the USDA will develop rules for mandatory labelling of bioengineered food. Here is the relevant definition in the law:

(1) The term 'bioengineering', and any similar term, as determined by the Secretary, with respect to a food, refers to a food—

> (A) that contains genetic material that has been modified through in vitro recombinant deoxyribonucleic acid (DNA) techniques; and

> (B) for which the modification could not otherwise be obtained through conventional breeding or found in nature.

As consumers we may want to know that our food is "natural," however, using this word is just substituting one misleading false dichotomy for another. You see, almost nothing we eat is as it occurred in nature prior to our tampering. In the delivering of food to supermarket shelves, there are a multitude of manufacturing techniques used, and drawing an arbitrary line somewhere makes no logical or scientific sense.

For example, there are thousands of crops on the market that are the creation of mutation breeding. Farmers use chemicals or radiation to promote mutations and then conduct a lot of trial and error to find the perfect mutation. Many neutral or potentially dangerous mutations are going to occur along the way as well, but using radioactivity to produce mutant crops is not considered genetic engineering and ironically is also acceptable as "organic."

Food Yoga

The concept of food yoga was born out a desire of mine to demystify the spiritual connection between humans and food. In my book, *FOOD YOGA – Nourishing Body, Mind & Soul* [40] I explain:

Rooted in Hindu tradition, the spiritual dimension of food yoga has meaning for people of all faiths. In Hinduism, all food is first offered to God – the very source of that food's creation. Such offerings can be elaborate rituals conducted with great fanfare using expensive paraphernalia and food ingredients, while other offerings may be humble gestures consisting of no more than fresh fruits and water. In all cases, however, it is the intention or the devotion of the aspirant that is foremost. Such offered food is considered pure, karma-free,[41] and spiritually nourishing. Hindus call this food *prasadam*, or the mercy of God.

Hinduism is a complex and varied belief system that accepts many gods and goddesses as emanating from a single source, *Brahman*, which is understood either as an impersonal, formless energy, as in the *Advaita* tradition, or as a dual (male/female) god in the form of *Lakshmi-Vishnu*, *Radha-Krishna*, or *Shiva-Shakti*, as in *Dvaita* traditions.

To the naturalist, the Goddess is simply "Mother Earth." After all, all food comes from the earth. Some currents of Neopaganism, in particular Wicca, have a concept of a single goddess and a single god who represent a united whole, glorified as the Lord and Lady (*Frey* and *Freya*, literally translated), with the Lord representing abundance and fertility and the Lady representing peace and love as well as vast powers of magic.

Whatever your belief, the fact that you are reading this book tells me that you may be open to accepting a higher power, and in your own unique way, you honor that higher presence.

My goal here is not to explore the entire subject of foodism, but rather to focus on its more divine aspects, beginning with an acceptance of a benevolent presence in our lives and evolving

---

[40] Published November 29, 2013 and available on Amazon
[41] Free of any negative reaction resulting from impious behavior.

to appreciating that presence through the offering of pure food, much the same as when you honor a friend in your home. Giving food is the most fundamental act of kindness a human can do, and eating food is one of the few things *all* humans have in common.

Food yoga springs from the belief that the kind of food we eat affects our consciousness and subsequent behaviors. According to the *Bhagavad-Gita, sattvic*[42] foods can be energetically purified by being offered in devotion, thereby raising one's consciousness. For this reason, food yogis avoid foods saturated with fear and suffering, such as meat, fish, eggs and commercial dairy products,[43] in favor of plant-based meals prepared with loving intention and made with fresh, organic ingredients. Moreover, if people prepare the food you eat with a polluted consciousness (e.g., disgruntled employees working in a dirty restaurant kitchen), you are sure to absorb negative psychic energies.

That food should be prepared and served in its purest possible form is central to the belief and practice of Food for Life Global,[44] a worldwide network of plant-based relief projects. Without adherence to this single principle, Food for Life Global would be no different than any other food relief agency. In fact, the non-profit sees itself more as a social change organization, with pure food as its preferred medium of expression.

At the root of all purity is an adherence to honesty and cleanliness, and both of these attributes can easily be applied to the food industry. The purest food for consumption is food that is energetically pure in *every* phase of its life cycle. When you look beyond the immediate gratification food offers and see food for what it truly is – energy – you tap into one of the greatest wonders of life and open the door to higher awareness.

---

[42] *Sattvic,* Sanskrit word meaning purity. For an object or food to be *sattvic,* it must be physically and energetically pure and lead to clarity and equanimity of mind while also being beneficial to the body.
[43] Unhomogenized and unpasteurized raw milk that comes from natural living, protected cows is considered to be in the mode of goodness.
[44] www.ffl.org

All the world's great spiritual traditions have elaborate food offering rituals carefully designed to expand consciousness. From the Holy Eucharist to Passover to *Diwali*, Christmas, Thanksgiving, and even the mushroom ceremonies of the Shamanic traditions – all use food as a means to represent or please the Divine and to expand the consciousness of their followers.

Food yoga is, in essence, a discipline that honors all spiritual paths by embracing their core teaching – that food in its most pure form is *divine* and therefore an excellent medium for expressing our unconditional love and purifying our consciousness.

Food yoga is both an art form and a science.

ART: The individual expression of love and devotion using food as the medium;

SCIENCE: An appreciation for the beauty and interconnectedness of all things, coupled with an unceasing awareness of the Energetic Source from which all things emanate.

AFFIRMATION 6

I honor my dependence on Mother Nature and try to intimately connect with her on a daily basis. This human form which I now use to express my spirit is her creation.

Maxim 7

Always Remember God

"It is impossible for that man to despair who remembers that his Helper is omnipotent."
- Jeremy Taylor

Omnipresence

According to all spiritual traditions, God is present in every part of the universe, including every atom of creation. As stated in the *Brahma-saṁhitā* (5.35), *aṇḍāntara-stha-paramāṇu-cayāntara-stham*: "The Lord is situated within the universe, within the heart of every living entity and also within the atom."

What was once considered religious naivety is now getting a serious look from leading noetic and quantum physicists, if but indirectly, thus alluding to the notion that there may indeed be a kind of universal consciousness that connected us all.

The *Bhagavat-Purana*[45] states:

> The Personality of Godhead is omnipresent by His diverse potencies everywhere, just as the power of electricity is distributed everywhere within space.

---

[45] Verse 1-13-10 (BBT)

Similarly, the Bible corroborates:

> God is omnipresent, filling heaven and earth with His character. "Am I only a God nearby," declares the Lord, "and not a God far away? Who can hide in secret places so that I cannot see them?" declares the Lord. "Do not I fill heaven and earth?" declares the Lord." (Jeremiah 23:23–24).[46]

God is not a localized being sitting upon His heavenly throne hidden from our vision. Nearness and distance make no difference in what God sees or does.

Vedic Scholar and guru, Srila Prabhupada comments: "There is nothing in the world with which the Lord is disconnected. The only thing we must learn is to excavate the source of connection and thus be linked with Him by offenseless service. We can be connected with Him by the transcendental sound representation of the Lord. The holy name of the Lord and the Lord Himself are identical, and one who chants the holy name of the Lord in an offenseless manner can at once realize that the Lord is present before him."

The "Universe"

In most of the modern literature on spirituality and consciousness, God is often referred to as the "Universe." It appears that not only has the mainstream thought embraced an impersonal worldview of divinity but that the hesitancy to talk about a personified Creator is a direct result of the atheistic and Luciferian dogma being marketed through pop culture.

Although for one in the beginning stages of spiritual awakening, there is no harm in seeing divinity in this way, much like a young child may not understand the full authority of the

---

[46] New International version (NIV)

president, however, those with greater awareness need take heed not to offend the personal form of the Lord.

Sadly, most people are afraid to talk of a personal form of God for fear of offending others in their social circle who may have a different religious belief or none at all. Ironically, it is such religious ambiguity that is killing spirituality and leading millions of people away from churches and mosques.

Personal And Impersonal

There are two basic schools of thought when it comes to the nature of God, impersonal and personal. The Vedic tradition defines them as the *Dvaita* and *Advaita* Vedanta schools of thought.

The *Dvaita*[47] Vedanta school believes that God[48] and the individual souls exist as independent, distinct realities. The *Dvaita* school contrasts with the other two major sub-schools of Vedanta, the *Advaita* Vedanta[49] which postulates that ultimate reality (Brahman) and human soul are identical and all reality is an interconnected oneness, and *Vishishtadvaita*[50] which presents that ultimate reality (Brahman) and human soul are different but with the potential to be identical.

The term *Dvaita* is a Sanskrit word that refers to any premise, where two principles (truths) or realities are theorized to exist simultaneously and independently.

Simultaneously One And Different

The great renaissance saint, philosopher, social reformer, and theological founder of the Hare Krishna movement, Sri Chaitanya Mahaprabhu (1486 - 1534), perfectly combined these two apparently disparate schools of thought into one all-encompassing

---

[47] Also known as "duality or dualism."

[48] Vishnu, or the supreme soul.

[49] Promoted by Adi Shankara, and also known as nondualism.

[50] Promoted by Ramanuja and also known as qualified nondualism.

111

philosophy known as *Achintya-Bheda-Abheda Tatva,* a school of Vedanta representing the philosophy of inconceivable one-ness and difference. In Sanskrit *achintya* means 'inconceivable,' *bheda* translates as 'difference,' *abheda* translates as 'non-difference' and *tattva* means 'truth.' The Gaudiya Vaishnava religious tradition employs the term in relation to the relationship of creation and the Creator (Vishnu).

The classic metaphor to explain this ideology is the simultaneous one-ness and difference of the sun globe and the rays of the sun. Both the rays of the sun and the sun globe cannot be separated since they represent our combined experience of the sun, however, no one can deny that they are also two separate phenomena.

The Essence Of All Spiritual Teachings

If we were to boil down all the teachings of the great saints and avatars of history, we could conceivably come away with two absolute statements: 1) The sound vibration of God's name is non-different from God and 2) unconditional service is the source of soul happiness.

Let's first talk about the power of God's name.

The Matthew 6:9 it states:

"Our Father who art in Heaven, hallowed be Thy name"[51]

and

"In the beginning was the Word, and the Word was with God, and the Word was God. (John 1:1).[52]

In the *Gita,* Krishna declares:

---

[51] 21st Century King James Version (KJ21)
[52] 21st Century King James Version (KJ21)

Of sacrifices I am the chanting of the holy names. (10.25)[53].

Similarly, the holy Quran states:

His are the most beautiful names. (59.24).

Praising or chanting the name of God or the Goddess is a special form of prayer. In many religions, the excellence of chanting the name(s) of God lies in the mystic syllables, which invoke God's purity and sovereign power. The various mantras in Hinduism and Buddhism – such as *Om, Hare Krishna, Namu-myo-ho-renge-kyo* or *Om Mane Padme Hum* – and the Roman Catholic practice of chanting on the Rosary all focus the mind on the spiritual plane and call forth its mystical elevating influence. In Christianity, prayers are offered in the name of Jesus Christ, who promises to do whatever is asked in faith. Indeed, in the hands of a great adept, the power of transcendental sound to initiate change could conceivably be unlimited, when we consider that creation itself was but the result of the Spoken Word!

When we intone names of God and cause the name to vibrate throughout our body and consciousness, we align our energy with that aspect of the divine creative intelligence represented by the name.

A source for divine names for those that resonate with the Judeo-Christian tradition is the ancient Hebrew *Qabala*. The ten names contained in the Tree of Life are the ten manifestations of the divine within the physical world. Three names, Amen, Hu, and Eheieh are considered particularly effective.

But to play the devil's advocate here, the extraordinary effects produced by such prayer may also be a result of a principle described as sympathetic vibration. For example, if one of the wires of a harp is made to vibrate vigorously, its movement will affect a sympathetic vibration in the strings of other harps placed around it, if they are tuned to the same pitch. In other words, there is nothing transcendental going on here, just strings harmonizing

---

[53] *Bhagavad-Gita As It Is.* (BBT)

by association. In any case, there is no doubt that after group prayer or focused group intention, powerful and transformative events do take place.

In the Jewish tradition, the explicit name of God is too holy to be uttered by the human tongue. In particular, the Tetragrammaton YHWH, which is translated "the Lord" in modern Bibles, is never to be spoken. To show respect, God is often referred to paraphrastically by such terms as the Lord, Heaven, G-d, the Name, and the King, the Almighty. Thus, to praise and bless the name of God, as in the psalm quoted here, means to extol God's greatness and mighty works without mentioning His sacred name. The intention is always one of invoking a pure sound, and thus, an auspicious outcome.

Of special mention are traditions of the many names of God that enumerate His many attributes. The Qur'an contains the ninety-nine most beautiful names of Allah, and from the *Mahabharata*[54] there is the *Vishnu sahasranama*,[55] "the thousand names of Vishnu." Each name eulogizes one of Vishnu's countless great attributes. To recite these names, it is said, is to give a magnificent description of the height, depth, and breadth of divinity.

In the Sikh *Adi Granth*[56] it is stated:

> *Contemplate solely the Name of God; fruitless are all other rituals.* [57]

> *The true essence, eternal is the Lord's Name.* [58]

Probably the most famous mantra of Buddhism is *Om*

---

[54] *Mahabharata* is one of the two major Sanskrit epics of ancient India, the other being the *Rāmāyana*.

[55] The *Vishnu sahasranama* as found in the Mahabharata is the most popular version of the 1,000 names of Vishnu.

[56] The Adi Granth, literally "the first book," is the early compilation of the Sikh Scriptures by Sri Guru Arjan Dev Ji, the fifth Sikh Guru, in 1604.

[57] Sikhism. *Adi Granth*, Suhi, M.1, p. 728.

[58] Sikhism. *Adi Granth*, Gauri Sukhmani 19, M.5, p. 289.

mani padme hum, the six-syllable mantra of the Bodhisattva of compassion, *Avalokiteshvara.*[59] This mantra is particularly associated with the four-armed *Shadakshari* form of *Avalokiteshvara*. The Dalai Lama is said to be an incarnation of *Avalokiteshvara*, and so his devotees especially revere the mantra.

Further, in the Contemplation Sutra of Amitayus[60], it is stated:

If there be anyone who commits evil deeds... let him utter the name "Buddha Amitayus" serenely and with voice uninterrupted; let him be continually thinking of Buddha until he has completed ten times the thought, repeating, "*Namu Amida Butsu*." On the strength of uttering Buddha's name, he will, during every repetition, expiate the sins. (3.30)

Throughout the Vaisnava literature, the Maha Mantra (*Hare Krishna, Hare Krishna, Krishna Krishna, Hare Hare, Hare Rama, Hare Rama, Rama Rama, Hare Hare*) is praised for its efficacy to instil devotion to God and purify the chanter of all worldly desires.

The second absolute truth is that unconditional service is what truly nourishes our spirit. We all have practical experience of this fact during the holidays when gifts are exchanged. Giving is always more pleasurable than receiving.

So why is this true, what is going on?

Each and every thing has an innate quality that defines that thing. For example, fire has the innate qualities of heat and light – you cannot separate these qualities from fire. Similarly, sugar has the innate quality of sweetness; chilies come with a burning sensation; ice is cold, diamonds are hard, water is wet and elephants are heavy, etc.

So according to all spiritual traditions, the innate quality of the soul is service. More specifically, unconditional service, in other words, service performed without expectation of return.

In verse, 1.2.6 of the *Śrīmad-Bhāgavatam*, it states:

---

[59] *Avalokiteshvara* (Tibetan: Chenrezig, Chinese: Guanyin).
[60] One of the three major Buddhist *sutras* found within the Pure Land branch of Mahayana Buddhism.

> The supreme occupation [dharma] for all humanity is that by which men can attain to loving devotional service unto the transcendent Lord. Such devotional service must be unmotivated and uninterrupted to completely satisfy the self.

In Romans 12:1 NIV it is stated:

> Therefore, I urge you, brothers and sisters, in view of God's mercy, to offer your bodies as a living sacrifice, holy and pleasing to God – this is your true and proper worship.

Furthermore, in Matthew 23:11 NIV it is written:

> The greatest among you will be your servant.

In the *Bhagavad-Gītā*, it is stated that only by devotional service can one understand the transcendental nature of the Supreme Lord and, after understanding Him perfectly in His transcendental position, enter into the kingdom of God.

Serving others comes natural to all of us, however, it is only when we direct that service to God unconditionally that the selfless act reaches its full potential – for service not only nourishes the soul – it prepares the path to developing a higher awareness and ultimately returning to our natural spiritual state.

The 9 Methods Of Bhakti

The *Bhāgavat Puruna* tells the story of the great saint Prahlāda[61] who overcame tremendous personal challenges to serve the Lord.

Prahlāda went on to become one of the greatest advocates and teachers of devotional service to Krishna and probably his most significant contribution to the devotional tradition was his 9 methods of bhakti (devotion)

---

[61] Prahlad belonged to the Kashyap gotra. He is described as a saintly boy from the Puranas known for his piety and bhakti to Lord Vishnu.

He described them as hearing and chanting about the transcendental holy name, form, qualities, paraphernalia and pastimes of Lord Vishnu, remembering them, serving the lotus feet of the Lord, offering the Lord respectful worship, offering prayers to the Lord, becoming His servant, considering the Lord one's best friend, and surrendering everything (body, mind and words) to the Lord. These nine processes are accepted as pure devotional service.

Prahlāda considered that one who dedicates their life to the service of God through these nine methods should be understood to be the wisest person.

The Importance Of Hearing

As you'll note, the first method of devotion prescribed by Prahlāda is hearing and for good reason, hearing is the sense that triggers an immediate shift in consciousness, more than any other sense.

When we sleep, the alarm clock is what arrests us into waking consciousness, similarly, if a burglar enters our home, we hear them first and respond accordingly. When a thunderstorm arrives, it is the crackling of the lightening that shocks people into action. When a mother is busy attending to her housework, the baby's cry can be heard over every other noise and will immediately grab the mother's attention.

In the same way, hearing transcendental sound has the effect of raising our consciousness – attuning it to a higher frequency of awareness.

Every living thing is attuned to a particular frequency of awareness that is suitable to the material condition (physical form and circumstance) that soul finds themselves in.

In fact, frequency or vibration is the fabric of the universe. Quantum physicists now believe that atoms are not actually physical but are made up of vortices of energy that are constantly whirling and vibrating, each one radiating its own unique energy signature, confirming the notion that we really are personified energy radiating our own unique energy signature.

Please understand, this is what leading scientist are saying, and although it is not exactly the same language as religious scholars, one would be a fool not to see the similarity of thought.

English astronomer Sir James Jeans[62] offers the following explanation:

> Today there is a wide measure of agreement, which on the physical side of science approaches almost to unanimity, that the stream of knowledge is heading towards a non-mechanical reality; the universe begins to look more like a great thought than like a great machine. Mind no longer appears as an accidental intruder into the realm of matter; we are beginning to suspect that we ought rather to hail it as the creator and governor of the realm of matter ...

Michael Talbot, author of *Mysticism and the New Physics* describes this as the "melding of physics and mysticism."

If you could observe the inner structure of an atom, you would find a tornado-like vortex, with a number of infinitely small energy vortices called quarks and photons. However, as you went deeper and deeper into the structure of the atom, you would observe emptiness, because the atom has no physical structure. Which means, our bodies and everything we observe in this physical creation also has no physical structure. Atoms are made out of invisible energies, they are not solid matter. We are also not solid matter.

Nikola Tesla once famously said, "If you want to find the secrets of the universe, think in terms of energy, frequency and vibration."

---

[62] Sir James Hopwood Jeans OM FRS MA DSc ScD LLD (1877–1946) was an English physicist, astronomer and mathematician.

Engaging Our Senses In Devotion

Prahlāda Maharaja is one of the greatest examples in recorded history of unconditional devotional service.

While being in his mother's womb, by good fortune, Prahlāda got to hear the devotional singing of the traveling saint, Narada Muni[63]. Prahlāda then learned about devotional service from Narada in his early childhood, and as a result, he became devoted towards Vishnu. His father, Hiranyakashipur had performed incredible austerities to receive a benediction from Lord Brahma, equating to immortality. Brahma had blessed the king to never be killed by a man or a beast; to not die inside or outside of a house; to not be killed on the land or in the sky; to not be killed by any weapon and to not die in the day or night.

Although feeling invincible, the king always felt threatened by the highly intelligent Lord Vishnu and so he despised Prahlāda's spiritual inclination and tried to discourage him. Despite several warnings from his father, Prahlāda continued to worship Vishnu so the envious king decided to destroy his only son and poison the boy, but miraculously, Prahlāda survived. Unrelenting, the king arranged for elephants to trample the boy, but Prahlāda still lived. He then put Prahlāda in a room filled with venomous snakes, but they made a bed for him with their bodies. Frustrated with his failure to take the boy's life, the king threw Prahlāda from a cliff but he was saved by Lord Vishnu who caught him before he hit the ground.

Holika, the sister of Hiranyakashipu, possessed the mystical power of immunity to fire, so Hiranyakashipu put Prahlāda on the lap of Holika as she sat on a pyre. Understanding the danger, Prahlāda prayed to Vishnu to keep him safe. Holika then burned to death while Prahlāda was left unscathed. This event was later celebrated as part of the Hindu festival of Holi.

---

[63] Narada is a Vedic sage, famous in Hindu traditions as a traveling musician and storyteller, who carries news and enlightening wisdom. He appears in a number of Hindu texts, notably the Mahabharata and the Ramayana, as well as in the Puranas.

After tolerating tremendous abuse from his father, Prahlāda was eventually rescued by Lord Narasiṁha, an avatar of Lord Vishnu in the form of a half man, half lion, who placed the king on his lap and killed him with his sharp nails at the entrance to his home at dusk, thus nullifying all of Hiranyakashipu's boons of immortality.

Prahlāda eventually became king of the daityas and attained a place in the abode of Vishnu (Vaikuntha) after his death.

Such examples of great souls overcoming hardship to express their devotion can be found in all the world's great spiritual traditions.

For example, St. Marguerite Bourgeoys was the first female saint from the Catholic Church in Canada. She was a Religious Sister who helped care for and educate many Native Americans and Canadian colonists who founded one of the first un-cloistered religious orders for women in the world, *The Congregation of Notre-Dame de Montreal.*

But in order to establish schools for immigrants and children in the 1600s, she faced grave dangers, including making three voyages to France, where she recruited Sisters to minister in hospitals. Marguerite also endured stark poverty, attacks from Native Americans and the dangers of what was then the Canadian wilderness.

Saint Josephine Bakhita was another saint whose dream of becoming a nun didn't come easily. Captured and enslaved in Sudan when she was only a child, Josephine was severely abused and suffered at the hands of her first four "owners."

To legally win her freedom and enter into the religious order, she had to find the courage to fight racism and injustice. After everything she had endured in her life, she finally became a Daughter of Charity in 1896 and went on to become a beloved nun who brought kindness and compassion to many children and adults.

The Story Of Joan

> *"One life is all we have and we live it as we believe in living it. But to sacrifice what you are and to live without belief, that is a fate more terrible than dying."*
> *– Joan of Arc*

Joan of Arc was born in 1412 Domremy, France to a poor family in a region suffering from a long conflict between England and France.

Joan of Arc achieved a remarkable achievement in her short life of 19 years. In particular, she embodied religious devotion with great bravery and humility, her life helped change the course of French history.

From an early age, Joan of Arc displayed a sensitive and religious temperament and appeared greatly committed to the service of God and the Blessed Mary.

From the age of twelve, she began to have mystical visions. In these visions, she said she felt the voice of God commanding her to renew the French nation. At her later trial, Joan of Arc said she felt these visions were as real seeing another person. The visions were often accompanied by light and the presence of saints such as St Michael and St Catherine.

> "I was thirteen when I had a Voice from God for my help and guidance. The first time that I heard this Voice, I was very much frightened; it was mid-day, in the summer, in my father's garden. – Joan of Arc from her trial transcript.

These visions inspired Joan. She would frequently go to confession and whenever she heard the bells for Mass she would stop all work and run to church.

Initially, Joan did not tell others about her visions and inner commandments but in May 1428 the divine messages urged her to seek an audience with Charles de Ponthieu the weak leader of the French.

In 1415, at the time of Joan's childhood, King Henry V of England had invaded France leaving the country seriously divided with a lack of national unity.

Under Charles de Ponthieu, the French were without direction and without a real leader, however, when Joan of Arc came to the court she impressed Charles so much with her passion and conviction that he appointed the 17-year-old peasant girl to command the French army and lead them into battle. Within a year, Joan of Arc had led the French army to victories at Orleans, Patay and Troyes. Many other towns were also liberated from English control and it allowed a triumphal entry into Dauphin for the coronation of King Charles VII on 17 July 1429.

For her exploits and leadership, Joan of Arc and her family were granted noble status. She also won the hearts of the French soldiers who looked up to Joan as an almost god-like leader. However, a year later Joan was captured by the Burgundian forces and sold to the English.

In order to humiliate the French army, the clergy decided to put her on trial for witchcraft. The leading church investigator was Pierre Cauchon – a staunch supporter of the British who hated Joan of Arc for her revival of French national pride. During her trial, she offered a warning to the Bishop about passing false judgement.

> "You say that you are my judge. I do not know if you
> are! But I tell you that you must take good care not to
> judge me wrongly, because you will put yourself in
> great danger. I warn you, so that if God punishes you
> for it, I would have done my duty by telling you!" –
> *Joan of Arc – Jeanne's warning to Bishop Cauchon*

The trial was initially held in public, but Joan's challenging responses disturbed her prosecutors.

> "They do not order me to disobey the Church, but
> God must be served first."

During cross-examination, her straightforward answers and modest demeanour gained her public sympathy.

Eventually, the trial was continued behind closed doors. It appears Joan was threatened with torture, though there is no evidence she was actually tortured.

As expected, Joan was found guilty and condemned to death by burning at the stake. Faced with such an overwhelming ordeal Joan broke down and confessed.

However, a week later she regained her strength and recanted her confession. This meant the penalty of execution by fire would be re-implemented. Witnesses recount she faced her ordeal with dignity. It is said that over 10,000 people came to see her execution by burning. Afterwards, her ashes were scattered in the Seine.

Twenty-six years later, the English were finally driven from Rouen, Joan was officially declared innocent and designated to be a martyr. Some 500 years later, she was canonised a saint in 1920 and remains the patron saint of France.

The Story Of Haridas Thakur

Another powerful example of overcoming adversity to serve the Lord is the example of the poor Muslim villager, known as Haridas Thakur.

Shri Haridas Thakur was born into the Muslim faith in the village of Buron, in Bangladesh in 1450. However, when he was a young man he became inspired by the Hindu scriptures and moved to the banks of Ganges at Fulia, near Shantipur, India to pursue his newfound spirituality.

The local brahmanas of Fulia were very pleased to see how Haridas constantly chanted the holy name of Krishna, and they used to come every day to sit with him. Gradually word spread to the Mohammedan minister who began to burn with malice and went to the local Mohammedan king (Kazi) to inform him, "Though he is Mohammedan, he behaves as a Hindu, therefore, he should be brought here for trial," the minister explained. The local king immediately asked that Haridas Thakur be brought before him for trial.

The Mohammedan King told Haridas, "Give up this foolish chanting of Hindu mantras and start singing the Kalma (prayer of the Mohammedans)."

Haridas Thakura replied, "The Supreme Lord is one, though His names might be different. The Hindu scriptures are the *Puranas* and the Muslim scripture is the Koran. Everyone acts as he is inspired by the Lord, as do I. Some meat-eaters become Hindus and some Hindus become meat-eaters, to worship the Lord. Oh Maharaja, how can you judge me for my spiritual preference?"

Hearing these defiant words of Haridas, the Kazi knew it would be necessary to punish him. The Kazi's assistant, Mulukpati pleaded, "My brother, just follow your own religion, then you will have nothing to worry about. Otherwise, you'll be punished."

Haridas answered, "Even if you cut my body into pieces, I will never give up the chanting of the holy name of Krishna."

Seeing Haridas's determination, the Kazi declared, "This man should be beaten in twenty-two market places. If he doesn't die after this, I will know that the learned gentleman speaks the truth."

Thus having heard the words of the Kazi, Mulukpati ordered that Haridas Thakura be whipped and beaten in twenty-two market places. Throughout the beatings, Haridas remembered the Lord by chanting "Krishna, Krishna", and miraculously, in the happiness of that remembrance, he didn't feel any bodily pain.

As the demoniac Hiranyakashipu tried in so many ways to kill his son Prahlāda but was unsuccessful, similarly, the Mohammedans who tried to brutalize Haridas were unable to do so. Haridas was immersed in the meditation of the holy name and thus gradually they could understand that he wasn't an ordinary person.

In great anxiety, the men humbly submitted to Haridas, "We can now understand that you are a genuine saintly person. No ordinary man could tolerate such suffering. But the Kazi will not understand this and he will now have our heads!" Hearing their frightened words Haridas entered into deep meditation and appeared lifeless.

The Mohammedans carried his body on their shoulders to Mulukpati, who believed he was dead. He then ordered that the body be thrown into the Ganges river. Haridas's body floated down the Ganges until it reached Fulia ghat, where he miraculously got out of the water and began to loudly chant again! Seeing the greatness of Haridas Thakura, now the Mulukpati became fearful. Along with the other Mohammedans he went to Haridas and begged for forgiveness. Now considering him to be a holy man, they all offered their salutations.

Haridas Thakur would chant for 23 hours of the day and most of the chanting took place in a hollowed out hole at the base of a large tree. Within the roots of this tree once lived a poisonous snake. Being fearful of this snake the local devotees couldn't remain there for very long and one day they mentioned their fear to Haridas. Seeing the distress of the devotees, Haridas Thakur told the snake, "My dear sir, if in fact you are residing here, then I am requesting that you please leave by tomorrow, otherwise I myself will have to leave here."

Hearing these words of Haridas, the snake immediately came out of its hole and went elsewhere.

Haridas Thakura lived at the same time as the great saint, Shri Chaitanya Mahaprabhu who preached the glories of the holy name and manifested as an avatar of Vishnu. He told Haridas, "Haridas, when those Mohammedans were beating you I was ready to destroy them with My Sudarshana Chakra, but as you were praying for their welfare I was unable to do anything.[64]

Therefore, I accepted their blows on My own body. Just see, the scars are still here on My body." Seeing those marks Haridasa fainted in ecstatic love.

---

[64] Chaitanya Bhagavat Madhya 10.42 (BBT)

The Example Of Ambarīṣa

Many millennia after the appearance of Prahlāda, the great King Ambarīṣa and son of Mandhatri ruled the planet in Treta yuga.

The great Vyasadev[65] the compiler of the Vedas, considers King Ambarīṣa to be the epitome of devotional service in that he successfully engaged all of his senses in the service of the Lord.

In the *Śrīmad-Bhāgavatam*, verses 9.4.18-20 it is described that King Ambarīṣa "first of all engaged his mind on the lotus feet of Lord Krishna; then, one after another, he engaged his words in describing the transcendental qualities of the Lord, his hands in mopping the temple of the Lord, his ears in hearing of the activities of the Lord, his eyes in seeing the transcendental forms of the Lord, his body in serving the devotees, his sense of smell in smelling the scents of the lotus flowers offered to the Lord, his tongue in tasting the sacred tulasī leaf offered at the lotus feet of the Lord, his legs in going to places of pilgrimage and the temple of the Lord, his head in offering obeisances unto the Lord, and his desires in executing the mission of the Lord. All these transcendental activities are quite befitting a pure devotee."

In the *Padma Purāṇa*, it is said that one should always remember Lord Vishnu and not forget Him at any moment. This is called *dhyāna*, or meditation and this state of consciousness is called samādhi, or trance.

A sincere devotee of God will try to mold their activities in such a way that they will constantly remember God.

AFFIRMATION 7

I am fully aware of my dependence on the divine grace of God. Nothing can happen without the will of the Lord and so I try to remember that in all my words and actions.

---

[65] Vyasadeva is generally considered the author of the *Mahabharata,* as well as a character in it and the scribe of both the *Vedas* and *Puranas*

Understanding Your Life Path

As I mentioned in Maxim 1, each of us has a life path and day number that is influencing and guiding us on our journey to spiritual awakening.

My day number is 4 and my life path or destiny number is 7. I explained the basic qualities of that combination but what about the other numbers?

I urge you to research this subject more in a book specifically focused on numerology but here is a basic introduction to the qualities of each day and destiny (ruling) number and hopefully it will give you some insight into what the ideal path is for you.

There are no destiny 1s simply because it is impossible to reduce any date to the number 1. There are no destiny 2s because if your birthday adds up to 29, 38 or 47, etc., you would reduce it to the master 11 and not 2.

Destiny 3

When we consider that 3 holds a commanding position on the mental plane of the numerology chart, specifically related to the left side of the brain, it shows us that such people are deeply analytical with sharp reasoning skills. Destiny 3 people's birth date adds up to 12, 21, 30, 39 or 48. However, 30 is the most powerful of destiny 3s, combining the number 3 with 0 (infinity)!

Because you emphasize the thinking side of life, it is clear that your primary purpose relates to your mental capabilities. You are an "intellectual" or the "sharp and witty" type. Your thought process dominates over your intuition and practical involvement, however, if your day number is 4 or 7 then you will have a nice balance of the planning and the practical. Your preferred way of expressing yourself is always related to being analytical, strategizing, planning or memorizing, even if the subject is trivial. You are socially adept and enjoy the spotlight and love life in all its aspects. Destiny 3s love to be the "joker" of their social circle.

Destiny 4

People born under this vibration are the most pragmatic and "hands-on." In a world where so much emphasis is based on material concerns, these people are usually easily satisfied. But there is much more to them than materialism. The number 4 is the center of the physical plane which rules health and pragmatism. They do well in all things related to the practical. Birthdates adding up to 13, 31, or 40 have a Ruling number of 4.

At this time in our soul evolution, we have to experience a human physical form and deal with all the challenges of material life. To deny this, as do many spiritualists, means that we may ignore the practical lessons and experiences that our soul needs to progress. Ruling 4s thrive on having the physical experience and need it in their early development. But as they mature, the natural tendency of these people is to elevate this expression to embrace the organizational aspect of this vibration, leading to broadening their love and awareness for the world.

Destiny 5

Typically, people with a ruling number 5 strive for freedom of expression and abhor any kind of constriction. You are highly sensitive and feel a strong need to express your feelings on all matters and in all situations, even when it may not be appropriate. But your caring nature and sincerity often covers for this tendency and your friends embrace your openness and soft heart. Birthdates adding up to 14,23,32, or 41 have a Ruling number of 5.

The mastery of self-expression is something everyone strives for, but ruling 5s have a natural flare for it. Writing, art, and music are common forms of self-expression and they help us to be more in touch with our higher self. Rulings 5s feel that the opportunity for self-expression is a birth right, however some do not understand the true purpose of this exercise, which is to constructively direct our lives. Freedom of expression is useless unless it is constructively directed.

Destiny 6

Ruling 6 people can be extreme in nature. They have the potential for tremendous creativity when living positive lives, but can fall into a deep dark cavern of sadness and worry when living negatively. The position of this number at the center of the Mind/ Intellectual plane while also being at the head of the *Arrow of Will* (4,5,6) gives Rulings 6 people extraordinary potential to envision and create brilliantly. Unfortunately, they rarely experience lasting success in their lives because of their tendency to worry about the future and not live in the "now." Birthdates adding up to 15,24,33, or 42 have a Ruling number of 6.

6 people excel over a wide range of creative expressions, from the home to the stage of world fame. Number 6 is the number of the divine feminine so Ruling 6s are very sensual by nature. They have a great responsibility for upholding culture and human affairs both of which require loving dedication. Although equipped to fulfil this promise many 6s become so identified with this responsibility that anxiety and worry take over them. They need to learn to master situations where their natural expression of care and creativity are welcomed, rather than allowing the situation to control them. The main lesson for 6s is to learn loving detachment, which will develop as they identify themselves and others as soul.

Destiny 7

7 people are known for their hardships, sacrifice and service mentality. They are teachers of life who love to share their experiences. If a 7 person chooses to devote their service to God, they can finish up their karma in one lifetime and move on. They are mysterious and resourceful people. Birthdates adding up to 16,25,34, or 43 have a Ruling number of 7.

When it is necessary for us to make a huge step forward in our spiritual progress, we will incarnate as a 7, because this is the number of intense learning through personal involvement. 7 people are gifted in their ability to share this learning with the world. Much of life's lessons come through physical expression and there is no better teacher of this than a 7 person who are by nature more philosophical than the other numbers.

Destiny 8

8 people regard independence as a birth right. They are by nature very complex and so many people find it hard to understand their motives. They possess wisdom and strength of character and so are often well suited for leadership. This leadership quality derives from 8 being at the head of the spiritual plane and at the middle of the arrow of activity (7,8,9). Ruling number 8 have birthdays adding up to 8,17,26, 35 or 44.

The most important aspect of love is being able to express it. For true love to be expressed there needs to be independence or free choice. Love cannot be forced. It is this desire for independence that is the core of what defines an 8 person. They are inherently personal and shun any idea of conformity or "oneness." However, one aspect of love is fluent expression of appreciation and it is this feature that 8 people sometimes struggle with. Therefore, an essential feature of their purpose in life is to transcend these limitations. 8 people make great progress once they learn to embrace the fact that appreciating others will not inhibit their independent voice, but will strengthen relationships and the confidence others have in them. This in turn makes 8 very wise counsels.

Destiny 9

Humanitarianism and big thinkers are often found as Ruling 9s. They are always ambitious, responsible and idealistic with a strong tendency to be right brain dominant. This right brain dominance helps them to think broadly and out of the box. Ruling number 9 have birthdays adding up to 9,18,27, 36 or 45.

9 is a powerful mind number evoking a powerful sense of responsibility in those that possess it. Such people are far better suited to art than science or to humanitarian and social services, rather than commercial. Many cultural leaders will be found with this number as well as the more serious or dramatic actors. Ruling 9s are all idealists at heart but not always the most practical people to work with, which is a major life lesson for them – translating their awe inspiring ideals into practical action. They also have a tendency to exaggerate which over time can make others not trust them.

Destiny 10

People with a Ruling 10 are some of the most adaptable, likeable and powerful people with potential for brilliant success when living positively. But when choosing to live negatively, they can flounder, feel lost and be very insecure and lead mediocre lives. Ruling number 10s have birthdays adding up to 10, 19, 28, 37 or 46.

10 is a powerful Sun number, so this number can inspire, empower and regenerate, or it can burn and wear down a person. Adaptability and adjustment are two key qualities of Ruling 10s. Their amazing flexibility can be of great help to their friends and colleagues in adjusting to life challenges. This natural ability leads many Ruling 10s to work in a variety of fields, but they are most effective when taking a pioneering position or work that requires a fearless attitude or risk.

10s express themselves best when allowed the freedom to do what they consider to be the "spice of life." They hate to be suppressed in any way or for their emotions to be minimized or hampered. They are drawn to professional sports, either actively or passively, or all kinds of entertainment. Because of their refined taste and eye for quality they make great interior designers, clothes designers, or chefs. They have a gift of the gab and so make great salespeople, fundraisers, business executives, planners, architects or real estate agents.

Destiny 11

An exceptionally high level of spirituality surrounds this ruling number, offering those born under it a unique potential for developing awareness of their higher self. Sadly, most people fail to live up to this potential and live rather ordinary lives. Birthdates adding up to 29, 38, or 47 have a Ruling number of 11.

Usually Ruling 11s will be found to be working to uplift spirituality and all kinds of personal growth. Whether you know it or not, you are highly intuitive and with only a little practice can cultivate great mental and spiritual powers. However, as like all things in life, your association is an important component to determine how successful you will be in realizing your full potential.

You are among the few people who are best equipped to guide humanity into the new age of enlightenment. To be born under the influence of 11 gives you a great sense of responsibility and this power should not be wasted frivolously. Again, the company you keep will have a great bearing on your success.

Destiny 22

This is the supreme master number in numerology and so the rare few (2 % of the population) that have this as their destiny number possess an almost unlimited potential to do tremendous things in life. However, there are two distinct 22s, the aware and the unaware. For those who by fate or bad karma do not realize their tremendous potential, they become lazy and indifferent and sometimes eccentric misfits. For those that are aware of their powerful potential, they can literally achieve anything they set their mind on. In other words, there are no "average" 22s. Birthdates adding up to 22 have a Ruling number of 22.

You are among the few people who are best equipped to guide humanity into the new age of enlightenment. To be born under the influence of 22 gives you amazing insight and the double power of the Moon to harness peaceful and brilliant outcomes. Again, the company you keep will have a great bearing on your success. You serve best from behind the scenes, although you prefer and are at your best when at the heart of management. 22s rarely like the limelight or starring role, however, in recent times this tendency has shifted with the urgency of enlightened leadership and 22s are putting themselves forward. It is important for them to feel respected and have cooperation.

The Day Numbers

Now that you know your destiny or ruling number, it is important to distinguish that with your day number, which is simply the day of your birth reduced to a single digit unless it is the number 11 or 22. Each day number has a corresponding ruling planet and set of qualities.

Day 1

Ruled by the Sun which has the qualities of pioneering, forcefulness, individuality, determination and positivity.

Day 2

Ruled by the Moon which has the qualities of peacefulness, diplomacy, intuition, foresightedness and balance.

Day 3

Ruled by Jupiter which has the qualities of sharp wittedness, analytical, jovialness, sociability and judgemental.

Day 4

Ruled by Rahu which has the qualities of pragmatism, groundedness, organized, materialistic, and a love for competition.

Day 5

Ruled by Mercury which has the qualities of communication, empathy, sentimentalism, compassion and friendship.

Day 6

Ruled by Venus which has the qualities of sexuality, thirst for notoriety, a love for home, creativity and academics.

Day 7

Ruled by Ketu which has the qualities of mysticism, a desire to teach, philosophizing, and charity.

Day 8

Ruled by Saturn which has the qualities of prosperity consciousness, leadership, compassion in action, a desire for individuality and religious outreach.

Day 9

Ruled by Mars which has the qualities of boldness, courage, idealism, responsibility and expanded thought.

Day 10

Ruled by the Sun, 10s are powerful, pioneering, risk-taking and bold.

Day 11

Ruled by double Suns which has the double power of the sun qualities with exceptional leadership qualities and courage.

Day 22

Ruled by double Moons which has the double qualities of the moon with exceptional intuition, compassion, serenity and refined taste.

How to Apply these 7 Maxims

Now that I have laid out the meaning and logic behind these maxims of soul happiness, it is now time for you to start applying them in your own life. You can only make so much progress with theory alone, at some point in time you have to dip your toes in the water and experience the new reality.

Let's summarise the maxims:

1. The Human Body is a Blessing
2. Death is Nothing to Fear
3. We are Absolute Consciousness
4. Evolution of Consciousness Begins When We Master Our Tongue
5. You Are A Creator
6. Connect with Mother Nature
7. Always Remember God

I think you'll agree that each one of the maxim is digestible. Starting with a positive foundation, we have first established the fact that the human form is indeed a great boon that should be appreciated. Next, when we consider our true nature as immutable energy (souls) then why should we ever fear death? We are not random accidents in a relative world, but are absolute consciousness expressing ourSelf through material forms. The key to unlocking our higher consciousness lays in mastering the functions of the tongue – eating and speaking. We should honor the body as a temple of the soul and therefore only consume foods and vocalize words that raise our awareness. Since our bodies consists of the same elements that make up nature, we should mold our life in such a way to always be connected to Mother Nature. Finally, as spiritual beings, we should know that this earth plane is not our true home but a place from which we can learn, evolve and springboard from to return home back to Godhead. Remembering the source of creation, God in whatever form feels right to you, is the most essential part of this evolution. Srila Rupa Goswami, a great Vaisnava scholar and saintly disciple of Shri Chaitanya Mahaprabhu, once stated: If one could boil down all the instructions of the *Vedas* into one concise statement it would be to *always remember Krishna and never forget him.*

About the Author

Australian-born Paul Rodney Turner, also known as the "Food Yogi," was a celibate monk for 14 years from age 19-33. He lived a simple life, including sleeping on the floor without a pillow, taking cold showers, rising at 3.30am every morning, meditating for 2 hours and studying the ancient Vedic literature of India.

Paul is a vegan chef, social entrepreneur, public speaker, numerologist, holistic life coach, spiritual guide and the international director of Food for Life Global, the world's largest food relief that serves up to 2 million plant-based meals daily.

He has traveled to 70 countries and cooked for presidents and leaders of the world. During Paul's travels, he visited three war zones, and in 2005, he led an international team of volunteers to set up makeshift kitchens in villages across Sri Lanka in response to the great Asian tsunami, where volunteers served freshly cooked vegan meals to hundreds of thousands.

He currently lives in the Andes Mountains of Colombia with his wife and son on their animal sanctuary.

References

BBT - Bhaktivedanta Book Trust Copyright ©1972 by His Divine Grace A.C. Bhaktivedanta Swami Prabhupada.

NIV - Holy Bible, New International Version ®, NIV® Copyright © 1973, 1978, 1984, 2011 by Biblica, Inc. ® Use by permission. All rights reserved worldwide.

KJ21 - 21st Century King James Version (KJ21) Copyright © 1994 by Deuel Enterprises, Inc.

Printed in the United States
By Bookmasters

Happiness is something we all crave for, whether in food, sex, entertainment, relationships, children, career, hobbies, or sleep. Happiness drives us, and indeed, it defines the quality of our life. One may have immense wealth, but if they are not happy, then mostly they have failed in life.

Without happiness, life loses its value. And with a decrease in satisfaction, we are witnessing an increase in suicide all over the world. In a world where mental and physical stimuli are in abundance, it seems inconceivable that anyone could be unhappy. Surely, everyone can find some form of happiness, but alas, many people fail and go through life sad and exasperated or hope against hope for some sliver of joy to miraculously appear over the horizon of their destiny.

Happiness is the nature of the spirit. The Vedanta-sutras states, *Anandamayo 'bhyāsāt* — "The soul is, by nature, full of joy." However, due to misidentifying our true self with matter, we lose touch with this natural blissful state and identify with the pain and suffering of a physical form.

The 7 Maxims of Soul Happiness will provide the key to unlock the door to a more blissful life.

Australian-born **Paul Rodney Turner**, also known as the "Food Yogi," was a celibate monk for 14 years from age 19-33. He lived a simple life, including sleeping on the floor without a pillow, taking cold showers, rising at 3.30am every morning, meditating for 2 hours and studying the ancient Vedic literature of India.

Paul is a vegan chef, social entrepreneur, public speaker, numerologist, holistic life coach, spiritual guide and the international director of Food for Life Global, the world's largest food relief that serves up to 2 million plant-based meals daily.

He has traveled to 70 countries and cooked for presidents and leaders of the world. During Paul's travels, he visited three war zones, and in 2005, he led an international team of volunteers to set up makeshift kitchens in villages across Sri Lanka in response to the great Asian tsunami, where volunteers served freshly cooked vegan meals to hundreds of thousands.

He currently lives in the Andes Mountains of Colombia with his wife and son on their animal sanctuary.

U.S. $11.99

ISBN 978-1-9822-2245-1
51199
9 781982 222451

BALBOA
PRESS
A DIVISION OF HAY HOUSE